FINDING GOD'S LOVE IN THE
MIDDLE OF THE MESS

from my
MESS
to His
MASTER
PIECE

JOY GRANT

ˈedəˌfī
EDIFI PUBLISHING

From My Mess to His Masterpiece
Finding God's love in the middle of the mess

Published by Edifi Publishing
3446 Winder Highway
Suite M195
Flowery Branch, GA 30542

info@edifipublishing.com
www.edifipublishing.com

Edited by Meg Redshaw and Ruth Woodson
Cover design & layout by Gloria Stella
Author photo by The Living Lenz

ISBN: 978-1-7339305-9-8

Printed and bound in the United States of America

10 9 8 7 6 5 4 3 2 1

To Michele and Timmy,
Your work on earth may be finished,
but your work in heaven has only just begun.

"However,
I consider my life
worth nothing to me;
my only aim is to
finish the Race
and
complete the task
the Lord Jesus has given me -
the task of testifying to the
good news of God's grace."
Acts 20:24 (NIV)

Acknowledgments

To my children and my grandchildren: that every chain from my life would not carry to theirs, but be broken; that they would see the glory and forgiveness of God at work in my life and in theirs; and that they would be blessed beyond measure for generations to come.

To every woman that I have had the privilege to serve and who has touched me as I volunteered in the outreach ministry of human trafficking: may your bonds be broken, your hearts be healed, and may you realize your full potential in Jesus Christ.

To the pastors and leaders of my church, Free Chapel, Gainesville, Georgia, to the pastors and leaders of the Atlanta Dream Center, and the ministry of Out of Darkness: thank you for seeing my potential and allowing me to be the hands and feet of Jesus.

To my sister and her husband who allowed me to stay with them and spend countless hours behind closed doors while I completed this book: a special thank you.

To Meg Redshaw: thank you for pouring your heart, soul, and time into helping with this book. You always touched my heart with your sweet spirit, and now I know why. "I asked God to send me an angel, and He replied, 'I already did.' Then, I remembered you."

To Ruth Woodson: thank you for taking your time to read and do the final edits of this book, especially for your scriptural wisdom.

To Robert and Gloria Stella: the real miracle of my testimony is the way God aligned our paths to meet and publish this book. Thank you. I am astounded by His work.

Contents

INTRODUCTION

*"If anyone wishes to come after Me, let him deny himself,
and take up his cross, and follow Me."*
Matthew 16:24 (NASB)

About five years ago, I asked God to allow me to share my testimony so that others would know how much they are worth to Him. I had spent some time ministering to women who were either recovering from or still caught in sex trafficking and exploitation. Not only did I learn from these women, but I also realized that God was healing me through them. I saw women who were rescued that had begun and even completed their journeys into rehabilitation go back to destructive habits. It was painful to watch. I wanted them to know that they were worth more than going back to the abuse they had suffered.

I began to plead with God for answers. What could be done to break and unbind their chains of destruction? I needed answers not only to share with them, but for myself. Already in my forties and divorced from a bad marriage, I found myself afraid to start a new relationship. I needed to know why I had shallow relationships all my life and why I repeated the same mistakes.

I was the product of a bad upbringing and of a society that says, "Do what you want to do, when you want to do it; party, have fun, have sex. If you get pregnant, again, do what you want: keep the baby, give it up for adoption, or have an abortion." Sadly, I have done all three. Living a life that the world says is okay can rob you not only of the love that you deserve, but the love that your children deserve. I did not know that then. I only knew that I wanted a relationship and to be loved. I did not have the right set of tools, morals, or foundation to find that love. Consequently, I fell many times. And so, God led me to write my testimony about how He set me free from the destructive patterns in my life so that others, too, can be free.

As I began to write I had questions, doubts, and fears. I did not want to look at the past, I wanted to continue to move forward. The past is a place that I have come far from and have forgotten about. Looking back made me feel stuck in a place that I did not want to be. It forced me to remember a time that was messed up, full of mistakes, and bad choices. I would much rather write about where I am today, a new creation in Christ on a solid foundation. I knew writing this would require a full reliance upon God and His strength.

As I prayed about this, God reminded me, "You asked to share your testimony, didn't you?" Our past is a part of our testimony. What we have walked through, where we have failed, and where God has picked us up. I hoped for a great end to my testimony before I shared it. What the world sees as a successful and happy ending: the house, the God-fearing husband, the new car, the financial stability. I now know that God does not see those "things" as success. My success is the strength and peace that passes understanding that I have in Jesus Christ. The peace that I want others to have. Through this process material things are no longer my priority; instead, as it says in Acts 20:24, my desire is to finish this race.

The purpose of this book is to share the answers that God has given me. I hope that my personal journey will save even just one life from the heartache and mistakes that I have made. My hope is that you will see yourself in some of these pages and find that you are not alone or the failure that you think you are. Most of all, I hope that you find the love of Jesus.

Proverbs 24:16 says, "Though the righteous fall seven times, they will rise again..." (NIV) I have fallen many times, and each time Jesus was there to pick me up. No matter how many times you have fallen, He is there for you.

MISTAKES & POOR CHOICES

Chapter 1

"I do not understand what I do.
For what I want to do I do not do, but what I hate I do."
Romans 7:15 (NIV)

I once heard someone say, "there are no mistakes, only poor choices." This struck me as a little judgmental and it made me curious to look up the definition of *"mistake."* A mistake is an action or judgement that is *misguided* or *wrong*. The definition of *"misguided"* is having or showing *faulty judgement* or *reasoning*. Basically, a mistake is a wrong or misguided decision based on faulty judgement or reasoning. Bad decisions, faulty judgement, mistakes, we all make them. In my opinion, a mistake and a poor choice are one in the same. The question is: what causes the basis of our judgement or our reasoning to become *"faulty?"*

I am not a psychologist; rather, I am a person who has made plenty of mistakes, poor choices, and faulty judgements. We have all made poor choices and mistakes at some point in our lives. Some of us have learned from our mistakes and not repeated them. Others, like myself, continued to repeat them not knowing why. You may find yourself asking God the same question. "Why do I repeat the same mistakes?" The answers I have found for myself may not be the same for you. But if you seek God, He will answer you just as He has answered me.

Do you find yourself making the same mistakes over and over again? Do you go to work, to church or just live life like everyone else and hide those mistakes? No matter how great the job, how wonderful the church or how nice the clothes, are you carrying the shame of those mistakes deep inside? That is how I lived most of my life.

Life is full of mistakes and poor choices. We make them every day. For example, you are in a hurry to get home after a long day. You know the speed limit is 55 mph, but you are going 75 mph. You see the blue lights in the rear-view mirror and your stomach sinks. Maybe you knew the speed limit and ignored it. Maybe you were just cruising along enjoying your music, not paying attention. Either way the consequence of that mistake, or poor choice, is going to be a ticket. It doesn't matter what you call it, it's going to hurt and then it's over.

However, there are mistakes and choices that affect our lives for a long time, some for a lifetime. These are the mistakes that affect not only us, but those around us. We make the same choices no matter how hard we try, knowing it is wrong. We try our best not to do it, but soon find ourselves doing it again.

Maybe you take the same drug over and over, knowing it will eventually kill you; or perhaps it is alcohol that is destroying your life and your relationships. Maybe it is both. Maybe you allow anger to take control of your relationships and you are abusive to your spouse. You try to stop on your own and you are sorry, but then you do it again. Maybe you are the victim in the abuse, caught in the cycle of violence. You try to leave, maybe you do, but you just go back; and you don't know why.

Growing up, I had no basis or foundation to understand what love, or a relationship should look like. So, as a young adult, I was like an empty soul moving from one person to another, none of whom cared for me. I depended on my outward appearance, but inside I was very empty and very broken. I had relationships hoping and longing for more, but "more" never came. I realize now just how empty I was and how little I thought that I deserved. I put no expectations on those I allowed to use me, even though I secretly hoped for more. Sadly, I thought these relationships were normal; so how could I change something that I did not see as wrong?

LAYING DOWN THE FEAR OF JUDGEMENT

I became pregnant five times out of wedlock in this lifestyle. Yes, five. Now if you decide to continue reading, this is where the judgement needs to be left. Judgement will stand in the way of hearing the message I am trying to share and what God wants to share through me. I have heard the sarcastic comments all my life, "didn't you take birth control" or "you were fertile weren't you?" It is easy to laugh at someone else's mistakes and to judge, but it is difficult to look at our own.

My mistakes may look different than your mistakes, but we all make them, and we can all hide them. If you were to meet me, you would never know my past unless I chose to tell you; but because God has called me to tell my story, my mistakes are revealed to you. This isn't so that you can judge me and my wrong doings, but so you can see the grace and mercy of God that is available to each and every one of us, no matter what we have done wrong. 1 Peter 4:8 says that we are covered by love, "Above all, love each other deeply, because love covers over a multitude of sins" (NIV).

I will be as brutally honest as I can with my story and lay my fears of judgement at Jesus' feet. My trust lies in Him, with the only purpose of giving Him all the Glory. My flesh wants to go on with life and forget the past which I did for a while. But now my spirit wants nothing more than to answer the call of Jesus on my life and to take up my cross and follow Him. I want to share how He has healed me, saved me, restored me, loved me and has become all that I need in this journey of life. I want this story to be all about Jesus and little about me. He is the husband I've always desired and the Father I never knew. I want Him to become all things for you.

It's never too late for
hope and for change.

You haven't gone too far;
you haven't done too much.

There is always
room for hope.

@joygrantofficial
#frommymesstohismasterpiece

NEVER TOO FAR GONE

My hope is that you will see how valuable you are and allow Jesus to change your life, just as He continues to change mine. I pray that you will find yourself on solid ground, no longer needing the things that are binding you. That you see yourself as He sees you, full of hope with a future. It is never too late for hope and for change. You haven't gone too far; you haven't done too much. There is always room for hope.

God is full of love and hope. He wants not only to bless you, but to set you free; to restore all that was stolen in your life. Deuteronomy 30:2-4 says, "(when) you have returned to the Lord your God and have listened to and obeyed His voice with all your heart and with all your soul, in accordance with everything that I am commanding you today, you and your children, then the Lord your God will restore your fortunes, and have compassion on you, and will gather you together again from all the peoples where He has scattered you. Even if any of your dispersed are at the ends of the earth, the Lord your God will gather you together from there, and from there He will bring you back" (AMP).

This is the God I know and serve and want you to know. He will have compassion on you and will go to the ends of the earth to restore you. He wants to know you, bless you, and heal you. He wants to return to you all that was stolen from you because of hurt, pain, or bad decisions made in your life. It does not matter to God if those things were brought on by someone else or our own doing. What matters to God is that you are His child, His creation, and He longs to give you hope and good things. There is nothing that you can do to stop His love for you; and there is nothing you have done that He will not forgive. As you read this book let Psalms 25:5 become your prayer, "Guide me in your truth and teach me, for you are God my Savior, and my hope is in you all day long" (NIV).

FOURTEEN AND PREGNANT

I became pregnant at only fourteen years old. By fifteen I gave birth to a son. I tried to keep him, but after four months gave him up for adoption to a family member. Why I became pregnant so young is something I pushed out of my mind until recent years. This experience set my life up for failing relationships. I took complete responsibility for what happened even though I realize now that it wasn't my fault. I carried the responsibility of getting pregnant, and I also carried the blame. It distorted my view of myself and of men, relationships, and what was expected from me.

It wasn't until I was an adult that God brought me back to the memory of losing my innocence at such a young age. I was taking a course at my church, little did I know that during these classes the Pastors and Leaders were praying that God would reveal anything that was hindering our walk with Him. One day before class as I was in prayer, God brought me back to a day I did not want to look at; one I thought I had forgotten. I did not understand why God brought me back there; but I had asked Him for answers, and He was giving them to me. When you ask God to do something, *He will do it.*

Being young and innocent, I didn't know what had happened to me. A boy that I had a crush on talked me into skipping school with him. He was a little older than me. I was 14, he was 16. He told me that there would be a party at our friend's house and all of our friends would be there. I hesitated, but I skipped school and went with him. It turned out to be just the two of us there. He got me into the bedroom and coaxed me onto the bed and held me down. I told him to stop, but he didn't. I had no idea what was happening to me. I wanted to tell my parents, but I was afraid. Instead, I asked a friend what it was that he did to me. Thinking that this was how you kept a boyfriend, I allowed it to continue. He would invite me to his house after school. I just wanted to hang out with him in the living room and watch tv. He would say we could, but only after we went to his bedroom. I would look up and stare out the window above his bed until it was over. We never did hang out and watch tv afterward, and I always felt terribly ashamed. This would happen while his parents were at work. There were a few times after it was over, his mother would come home. I was always too afraid to come out of the bedroom. I remember eating dinner with them a few times. I would never speak at the table because I was so ashamed of what had happened. Growing up, my father always called me "the shy one." It wasn't that I was shy, it was that I was afraid to talk. This was no different. One time his mother asked me what was wrong, why I never talked; but I couldn't answer. I just shrugged my shoulders and said I didn't know. This continued until I became pregnant.

The sad thing is, I didn't know that this was how you got pregnant. I don't know why I was so naive at 14, but I was. I think growing up as I did, really sheltered and alone, I just didn't know and was not taught. I was still playing with Barbies at twelve and thirteen years old. The only reason I stopped playing with them was because a girl made fun of me. My sister who was 16 at the time had gotten pregnant. I asked her how she got pregnant, she told me it was by what me and the boy were doing. I sat down on the floor in our bedroom when she told me that and made a vow to myself, "I will never let him do that to me again. I'm going to be good and stay in my room and do my schoolwork." The only problem was that it was too late. I was already pregnant, and I didn't know it.

I began cutting my wrists while this was going on. There was no social term for it like "cutter" at the time. I would slice my wrists in the bathroom at home with a razor blade, each time a little deeper. I would wear long sleeves to school to hide my wounds and scars. Kids at school would ask me what happened, and I would just ignore them. There was something about "seeing" and feeling the external pain that made my internal pain more bearable. I felt I deserved the pain. Life at home was not any easier. In many ways between what I was experiencing with this boy and my home life, I did want to die.

CONFORMING TO A PATTERN

"Do not conform to the pattern of this world,
but be transformed by the renewing of your mind."
Romans 12:2 (NIV)

This experience started a very painful pattern in my life that continued until my late 30s. My mind believed that giving yourself over in a sexual way was love. You did what was expected first and then hoped for more: you hoped to "hang out and watch tv." I hoped throughout life for love, dates, movies, flowers, candy, engagement rings, weddings, all of which never came. As difficult as giving birth and having a baby were, it was the expectations about sex that had the more negative impact on me. I believe I did have "puppy love" feelings for the father and I thought I was in love. I know that there are successful couples who meet at a young age and are happily married. So, I want to say here that it is not the feelings that I had or thought I had, or even having my son that affected me. It was believing that I had to do something in order to be loved.

THE PROCESS OF TRANSFORMATION

Romans 12:2 says, "Do not conform to the pattern of this world but be transformed by the renewing of your mind. Then you will be able to test and approve what God's will is--his good, pleasing and perfect will" (NIV).

I did not know it then, but at 14 years old, I had "conformed to a pattern." It would not be until later in life that I allowed God to renew my mind and break this pattern of giving myself away for the hope of love.

It says in this scripture that we will conform to a *pattern* if we do not allow God to transform our minds. The patterns of abuse, neglect, addiction, discouragement, depression, anger, violence, etc., will be repeated if we do not find healing in the transformation of our minds through the love of Jesus Christ. Transformation comes through the reading of His word and believing what the word says about us. Transformation begins by practicing His word and giving our minds over to the spirit of God to become more like Him.

Romans 8: 5-6 says, "Those who live according to the flesh have their minds set on what the flesh desires; but those who live in accordance with the Spirit have their minds set on what the Spirit desires. The mind governed by the flesh is death, but the mind governed by the Spirit is life and peace" (NIV). Giving our mind over to Christ and allowing Him to "govern" our thinking brings us life and peace. There isn't much in life that can shake me now. We can strive daily to have the "mind of Christ: the mind of hope and peace.

NOT GOOD ENOUGH FOR GOD

"All have sinned and fall short of the glory of God."
Romans 3:23 (NIV)

The way my pregnancy was handled by some of the adults around me was damaging. The boy's mother took me to an abortionist. I did not know where we were going. I was told not to worry; we were going to someone who could "make your period come back." This was in the mid-1970s, and I didn't know anything about abortions. I just knew that I was afraid; and the "doctor" who examined me sent me away, saying that I was "too far along." I remember the boy's mom and brothers who had driven me there being so upset when the doctor told them I was too far along. I was so confused; I didn't understand why they were upset. Even at that moment, I didn't realize I was at an abortionist, or what it was; nor did I fully realize that what I was carrying was a baby. A human life.

Months later, after trying to hide my pregnancy, my father found out. He, too, did the same thing. He took me to see one of his "doctors" telling me it was for a checkup. Again, it was an abortionist. I was about 5 months along. Thankfully, this doctor was kind. He showed me compassion and told me the truth about why I was there. He explained to me how the abortion would be done. It would be a saline abortion. The baby would die a horrible death inside of me, and I would give birth to a dead child. He explained that it was up to me. By now I knew it was a baby inside of me and cried. I said no and left the room. My father was livid.

After having my son, I tried to keep him; but life at home was very difficult. I had turned 15 by then. I knew that I did not want my child to be raised like I was raised. The last straw was when my father threw a telephone at me, nearly hitting me in the head while I was holding my son. I packed up the baby and myself to run away, knowing I had no place to go. I knew I had to make a decision. So, hoping for a better life for my son, I contacted a family member who adopted him.

Giving up my son was a painful decision for my young mind. It was a loss that was unbearable for a girl who was a child herself. It was hard on my mother, too. Growing up I was always protective of my mother. I loved her very much. It hurt me to see her cry and I felt helpless in my decision. There was no one to help us through that pain. My parents just weren't capable and even though they should have taught me better in life, I have forgiven them.

After the adoption, I went back to high school and tried to be a normal student. It was only the beginning of my sophomore year. Here I began another pattern in my life of trying to be "good" on my own. I did not date anyone in school. I was not interested.

As a junior I went to prom with someone who, of course, dumped me because I would not have sex with him. I stayed strong on my own, not dating until my senior year. Then a girl started hounding me every time she saw me in the hall. Each time she saw me she would approach me about a new boy who wanted to date me. I was persistent in telling her no, that I was not interested. She was more persistent, to the point that I gave in just to get her to leave me alone. I met him and we began dating. By now it seemed that having sex with dating was normal. It was what you did and by graduation I found myself pregnant again. I now knew of girls at school who were having abortions, some multiple abortions. I already had a baby and so to me it was wrong. As afraid as I was to be pregnant again; I was secretly happy that I would have a baby to hold after losing my son. This began a pattern of making up for loss that spiraled out of control in my life.

"YOU'RE PREGNANT? I'M SORRY. YOU JUST WON'T FIT IN..."
After graduating high school, I moved to California to live with my sister and her husband. There my daughter was born. Not long after moving and while I was pregnant, a pastor from a local church came to visit us. He told us about their youth group. I didn't know what a youth group was at the time. I had never heard of one, but I was excited to join. When he was leaving, I walked outside with him and told him that I was pregnant.

He looked at me and said, "You're pregnant? I'm sorry, you just won't fit in," and he walked away. I stood there in shock and watched as he walked away from me. I was devastated and I cried for days. I was tormented with nightmares after that. I became very angry and thought if that is how God is, someone who would turn his back and walk away from me, then I want nothing to do with him.

It is sad looking back. This pastor had the chance to make a difference in my life. Instead, he judged me harshly and it affected me deeply. Never miss the chance to love someone into God's grace; and be careful that you do not judge. Matthew 7:1-2 says, "Do not judge, or you too will be judged. For in the same way you judge others, you will be judged, and with the measure you use, it will be measured to you" (NIV). I know I will have the chance to meet this pastor again in heaven and tell him it's okay, because I now know how deep Jesus' love is for me and no one can take that away. Never allow someone else's view of you to turn you away from God. God is a pursuer of love, and He is pursuing you. He never gave up on me. God was with me then and made He himself known many times as I ran from Him. I wish I knew then just how much He loved me. He loved me then and He loves me now. He loves you now.

GOD LOVES DEEPER
Ephesians 3:16-18 says, "I pray that out of His glorious riches He may strengthen you with power through His Spirit in your inner being, so that Christ may dwell in your hearts through faith. And I pray that you, being rooted and established in love, may have power, together with all the Lord's holy people, to grasp how wide and long and high and deep is the love of Christ, and to know this love that surpasses knowledge - that you may be filled to measure of all the fullness of God" (NIV).

No matter what others say or do to us, God loves us. People's opinions do not affect His love for us. As a matter of fact, I believe that the negative opinions of others cause Him to love us and pursue us even more. He wants you to know how much He loves you and He does not think the same as those who judge you. He loves you so deeply that you cannot grasp how *wide* and *long* and *high* and *deep* His love is for you!

Chapter 1

STUDY GUIDE

REFLECT Is there a habit or an addiction that you struggle with that you cannot conquer on your own?

Do you believe that Jesus has provided the way to free you from that habit or addiction?

What are some of the hurts or disappointments from your past that you believe are affecting you now?

READ Psalms 25:5 "Guide me in your truth and teach me, for you are God my Savior, and my hope is in you all day long."

Romans 12:2 "Do not conform to the pattern of this world but be transformed by the renewing of your mind. Then you will be able to test and approve what God's will is--his good, pleasing and perfect will."

Romans 8: 5-6 "Those who live according to the flesh have their minds set on what the flesh desires; but those who live in accordance with the Spirit have their minds set on what the Spirit desires. The mind governed by the flesh is death, but the mind governed by the Spirit is life and peace."

Ephesians 3:16-18 "I pray that out of His glorious riches He may strengthen you with power through His Spirit in your inner being, so that Christ may dwell in your hearts through faith. And I pray that you, being rooted and established in love, may have power, together with all the Lord's holy people, to grasp how wide and long and high and deep is the love of Christ, and to know this love that surpasses knowledge - that you may be filled to measure of all the fullness of God."

DECLARE I can be set free from the negative patterns and addictions formed in my life. Jesus has provided the way for me through the reading of His word and by practicing daily what He teaches me.

PRAY God, please bring to my mind any habit or addiction that is standing in the way of my relationship with you. Help me to understand that you love me and want the best for me. Renew my mind as I pray and study your word. Forgive me for _____, I give it to you. Thank you for giving me the strength to overcome and awareness that you do not judge me. Thank you that you love me enough to see me change and want the best for my life. In Jesus' name I pray. Amen.

THE IMAGE OF A FATHER
Chapter 2

"See what great love the Father has lavished on us,
that we should be called children of God!"
1 John 3:1 (NIV)

God is a good Father who wants to bless you far above all that you can imagine or think. It is hard to relate to God as a good father if you don't have an image of what a good father looks like. My dad was the best father he knew how to be; but he was a hurt and broken man. I grew up with abuse in my home and a very dark childhood. My dad was emotionally absent in our lives; except for anger, the only other emotion he showed was cold, dead silence. I never knew what to expect. The tension was always thick not knowing what would break that silence with an explosion. I felt happy and free when he was at work, but when he would come through the door I would retreat to my room. I grew up in my room as a little girl and as a teenager tried to stay away from the fighting between my parents.

I was not taught about Jesus, but He somehow made Himself known to me. My father had a very large Bible and in it were beautiful prints. As I looked through his Bible, I was always fascinated by the pictures of Jesus. One print in particular stood out to me; it was Jesus praying at the rock. I would sit in my room alone for hours drawing that picture. There was comfort in seeing Jesus in that print. Even though I didn't really know who He was, His image brought me peace.

Eventually, one of my older sisters brought my sister and I to church. I was about 10, my sister about 12. I remember the Pastor from that church to this day, his name was Pastor Lang. He came to visit us one evening at our apartment in Chicago. He prayed with both my sister and I and led us to accept Jesus into our hearts. We were both baptized at his church. The night that he prayed with me, I asked him if I could go and live with him. I remember how sad he looked when he explained that I couldn't. Even then, as a little girl I was searching for a father.

That was my only experience going to church as a child, but I am thankful for it. We never went to church; we had no vacations, no going out to eat as a family. My mother occasionally took us to a movie, but never as a family. We had no friends over to play, no birthday parties, no joy. When dad came home from work my sister and I would hide in our room waiting for the fights to break out. As a teenager I did not have friends over. I was too afraid and embarrassed because of how my father acted; cold and silent.

The only conversations with my father were on the cusp of emotional abuse. He kept me up many school nights until one or two o'clock in the morning forcing me to listen to stories of his troubled past. He grew up in an orphanage. Both he and his brother were left there by his mother. His mother came back when she was able to and took his brother home but left my father there. It scarred him for life. It was such a sad story. He had every right to be hurt, but he never knew how to get past his pain. So, he became what he knew: absent in mind and emotion, hurting those around him.

My desire to see any happiness in my parents was so strong that I would sit and wait for my father to laugh while he watched TV. Work and television were his life, I suppose television was his escape. I wouldn't watch the TV, I would watch him, and wait...wait for him to laugh or smile. I was so hungry to see any sign of happiness. If he would laugh at anything on the TV it made me happy.

The image of my father was so bad that I lived my adult life believing that having a husband was not important. I did not want anyone in my life like my dad, and I did not want my children to have a bad father in the home. So, if I got pregnant, I thought I would be perfectly fine raising my children on my own.

WITHOUT GOD, HISTORY REPEATS ITSELF

The way we see our father treat our mother is not only important in our childhood but can affect our choice of a spouse. My father called my mother terrible names. My mother was from Guatemala and was Spanish and Italian by nationality. She came to the United States as an immigrant with her mother and siblings when she was six years old. She became a naturalized citizen and at the time arrived in New York through Ellis Island. Sadly, my father used this against her throughout their marriage calling her names regarding her ethnicity and threatening to "send her back" to Guatemala. The saying "sticks and stones may break our bones, but names will never hurt us" is not true. Hearing these things hurt my mother and us children deeply. After all, we came from our mother and we reasoned that if she is these things, then we must be these things, too. Proverbs 18:21 says that the power of life and death are in the tongue. Our words can be used as weapons or used as a means of healing.

Sadly, as a child I began to believe that if I wasn't worth my father's time, love or attention; then I must not be worth it to anyone else. When you believe this about yourself, you will accept what *feels* like love from anyone; and when I did finally marry, my husband affirmed this. He constantly told me how little I was worth. I married someone who was not only just like my father, but worse. History will often repeat itself in you and your children if you do not allow God to change you.

I loved my mother and father very much. They are both deceased now. My father came from a hurt and broken background. My mother was loved by her mother but abandoned by her father. After immigrating to the United States, she was teased and bullied because she could not speak English. She only made it to the third grade, and she put herself down for it her entire life. She was beautiful, gorgeous. She met my father when she was only 18 and ran away with him. He was 10 years older than her, but he lied about his age and did not tell her that. Just like the bullies on the school playground, he put her down and called her terrible names. Harmful patterns continued in both of their lives. Neither one of them is to blame. They were walking wounded, and then they met each other. This is what can happen when we do not go to God for healing.

Hurtful and harmful behavior continues from those before us, to us and to our children. We must do everything we can to allow Jesus to break this cycle. The work that you will see being done in this book is the work that was done through Jesus to bring freedom to my life and, as a result, my children's lives. When we allow God to set us free it can mean future freedom for not only your children, but generations to come!

PROMISCUOUS

"Flee sexual immorality. Every sin that a man does is outside the body, but he who commits sexual immorality sins against his own body."
1 Corinthians 6:18 (KJV)

There was one person in my life that I admired as a father figure. He was a good example to me of what a father should be. He loved his family and treated them well. When I was nineteen and after having my daughter, he was giving me a ride somewhere. It was just he and I alone in the car and he began to graphically explain a very sexual dream he had of me. I was angry and heartbroken. He, too, shattered my image of a father. In that very moment alone in the car, I gave up and gave into the lie that I was worthless except for sex. I wanted better in my life but had already been pregnant twice. I stopped caring and became very promiscuous. This would open the door for one of the worst memories in my life, and that is abortion.

Living in California and on one of my first jobs, I worked with a woman who was older than me. I was young and just wandering through life; learning everything the hard way. I was vulnerable, but still hoping for a better way. I wanted to be an artist, always dreaming of ways to use my talent but found myself stuck in a rut with a job that I did not like. I had even met a man who was a designer for a major theme park in the area. I showed him my artwork, my art was good. But this man, too, only wanted to try and take advantage of me. I was a good target, for men and women alike. A young, pretty girl with no direction.

This woman at work befriended me. She taught me how to dance on tables at bars, she was divorced with three children. She asked me to become a roommate at a house with her, so I did. She was sleeping with a married man. She asked me if I ever had a one-night stand. I didn't know what that was, and she told me.

THE WAR FOR YOUR SOUL

If there is anything you can learn from reading this testimony of mine it is this: God sees you, He is there for you. If you are lonely and vulnerable, if you see yourself in me already, stop and pray. Life is different for me now. Find a good solid church. Get involved no matter who says you can't, God says you can. Don't stop, keep looking until you find that church you are comfortable in. I believe you will find a church where people will love you just as you are.

Not only does God see you, but Satan sees you. 1 Peter 5:8 says, "Be sober, be vigilant; because your adversary the devil walks about like a roaring lion, seeking whom he may devour" (NKJV). Satan wants to "devour" you and your life. God is real and the devil is real. The devil will do everything and anything he can to keep you away from God. When you are vulnerable and out there, the devil is going to send someone or something to distract you and to get you off the right path. He may even try to destroy you. He doesn't want you to know that God has a place for you. He wants you to feel as rejected as I did the day that pastor walked away from me. He wants you to rebel like I did after that experience alone in the car. He wants to pull you down as deep and as dark as he possibly can. I know this because that is exactly what he did to me.

There is a war going on for your soul. 2 Chronicles 16:9 says, "For the eyes of the Lord move to and fro throughout the earth so that He may support those whose heart is completely His. You have acted foolishly in this; therefore, from now on you will have wars" (AMP). God's eyes go to and fro looking for us, to support us, and love us. When we reject him and run from Him and His ways, when we "act foolishly," we will have wars. Wars in our soul and for our soul with the devil who seeks to devour us.

I didn't have these teachings or the foundation of Christ that I needed to understand what temptations were coming my way. But now that you have read this, you do. If there is just one of you out there that can be saved from what I walked into, then bearing my soul and my past to you is worth it.

SEARCHING THROUGH THE PAST

"When the righteous cry for help, the Lord hears and delivers them out of all their troubles"
Psalms 34:17 (ESV)

Looking back, I began to question whether as a child I may have been sexually abused. There was emotional abuse but nothing sexual that I can recall. I've prayed and asked God to reveal any memories that may have started this darkness in my life so there can be complete healing. Even though it was not a pretty childhood, I cannot remember any sexual abuse from my father towards me; but I do know that I knew more than I should. It seemed like the devil was after me from a young age. I was surrounded, it seems, by inappropriate incidents.

I remember going to a friend's apartment in Chicago and her mother was laying with her bottom half nude on a bed. The bedroom was in an area that for some reason we had to walk through. I remember her asking us to get in bed with her and being afraid. There was another time I was playing in the back alley of Chicago where some construction was going on. It was like a giant sand pit. Digging through the sand with some other children we found very graphic pornography. These were actual enlarged photographs. Why they were there, I do not know. Another time while walking through the alley with a friend who lived in my apartment building, we were approached by a man. He asked us to go into an abandoned building with him to see a puppy. I said no and told her not to go, but she did. I ran home to tell her mother, but by then it was too late. She was raped; we were about 9 years old.

I remember being very small, maybe about six or seven and playing under the Christmas tree with Ken and Barbie. I was hiding under the tree and I had them perform the act of sex. I was caught by my older sister who proclaimed, "What are you doing? How do you know about that?" I only remember that it was a "secret" how I knew; but to this day, no matter how hard I have prayed, I cannot remember what that secret was. Maybe it was the pornography I saw; I don't really know.

There was one other incident with a neighbor when I was around 10 or 11 years old. My parents, for whatever reason, thought it would be okay for me to babysit at a neighbor's apartment. I remember the lady. I used to love to go to her apartment upstairs and get sweet and spicy little crackers. They were so good. She talked my mother into letting me sit with her kids while she and her husband went out. I remember my mother saying I was too young. I thought I was too young, too, and I didn't want to do it. The lady convinced my mother that it would be okay saying that they live right upstairs, and my mother could check on me.

I did watch her children and it got late and I fell asleep in their bed. I was too little, too young. I woke up to what I felt was being smothered. The man was on top of me, touching me and kissing me. I couldn't breathe. I remember crying and telling him to stop. I looked over to see the woman in the doorway watching. All I can remember is looking at her crying and saying I wanted to go home. I can still see her silhouette in the doorway, the bathroom light shining behind her. After watching she finally told him that was enough, and he got off of me. I ran back to our apartment and told my father. I remember being upset, and my father going upstairs angry.

There were other incidents that I can recall. But I don't think any of them affected my life as deeply as the lack of relationship with my father; and the emotional and physical abuse I witnessed towards us and my mother.

21

Satan wants to
pull you away
because
he knows how
valuable you are
to God
and that
God has a plan
and purpose
for your life.

DESPERATE FOR A FATHER'S LOVE

However, the worst memory is of a phone call I received from my father. It wasn't long after that experience in the car when I was twenty. I was still in California and my father called me from Georgia. He began to talk about very sexual and explicit things to me on the phone. Things that he wanted to do to me, and that he wanted me to do to him. I was shocked, embarrassed, and sick to my stomach; but I didn't stop him. I listened and for a moment entertained what he was saying. He said he was going to call me back the next night and do it again and I agreed. He called again, and I allowed the phone call to happen. I had already given into the idea that I was worth only sex, and that sex was love. I was so desperate for my father's love; I was even willing to accept this. It felt wrong, but it *also felt like he was showing me love.*

My roommate, the lady I worked with, overheard the last conversation with him and asked me who I was talking to. I told her it was my father. She said it was wrong for my father to talk to me like that, and I needed to tell him to stop. So, when he called to do it again, I told him I would not take these calls from him anymore. I am thankful now to this day that my father was thousands of miles from me. I don't know what would have happened if he was in the same house at the time.

Can you see the progression of things that lined up in my life? It was a perfect set up. The longing for a father, early pregnancies, the rejection by a pastor, the sexualization of my image by those around me and my own father; these things were the perfect storm for Satan to step in and pull me away from God. Satan wants to pull you away because he knows how valuable you are to God; and that God has a plan and purpose for your life. A plan for good, not for evil. Satan needs to pull every person away from God that he can. He needs to do this because each person has a perfect will from God to win souls for Christ. Satan wants not only your soul, but the souls of anyone you would influence to follow Christ.

YOU ARE A TEMPLE

I want to stop now and say here that if you are being sexually abused by anyone, get help. It is not okay for anyone to hurt you, take advantage of you in any way, sexually, emotionally, physically, or verbally. Tell someone that you trust. I don't care who they are or how old they are, it is not okay. Your body is precious, your mind is precious, your emotions are precious, you are precious to God. Your body is a temple of God's Holy Spirit. It says so in 1 Corinthians 6:19-20, "Do you not know that your bodies are temples of the Holy Spirit, who is in you, whom you have received from God? You are not your own; you were bought at a price. Therefore honor God with your bodies" (NIV).

You are precious enough to be called a temple, God's temple. Do not allow anyone to defile the house of God; the house that is you. I can tell you that anyone who dares to defile you and your temple will face the wrath of God. Jesus showed His anger towards those who defiled His father's temple in John 2:13-16, "When it was almost time for the Jewish Passover, Jesus went up to Jerusalem. In the temple courts he found people selling cattle, sheep and doves, and others sitting at tables exchanging money. So, he made a whip out of cords, and drove all from the temple courts, both sheep and cattle; he scattered the coins of the money changers and overturned their tables. To those who sold doves he said, 'Get these out of here! Stop turning my Father's house into a market!'" (NIV). Just as Jesus drove out the money changers from His Father's temple, He will drive out those abusing you; and He will give you the power to drive them out through prayer.

A temple is a beautiful place of honor and worship. We are not to worship our body, but to treat it as a valuable place that God's spirit dwells. If God's spirit dwells within you, then you are His temple and worthy of being treated in an honorable and respectful way.

Chapter 2
STUDY GUIDE

REFLECT As you grew up, did you have a good father in your household?

How do you think the influence of your father affects your decisions today?

Do you believe that God is a good Father and that He loves you as His own child?

If you don't believe it, what can you do to change your perspective of God?

READ 1 John 3:1 "See what great love the Father has lavished on us, that we should be called children of God!"

Psalms 34:17 "When the righteous cry for help, the Lord hears and delivers them out of all their troubles."

1 Corinthians 6:19-20 "Do you not know that your bodies are temples of the Holy Spirit, who is in you, whom you have received from God? You are not your own; you were bought at a price. Therefore, honor God with your bodies."

DECLARE I am a temple of God's Holy Spirit, created as a place where God can dwell. My past influences and decisions do not change the fact that God wants to live in me and direct me, just as a Father lovingly directs His child. He loves me and wants the best for me.

PRAY Father, help me to see you as a good Father and to see myself as your child. Change my desires from pleasing myself to pleasing you. Please break any harmful cycle that my father, or lack of a father, has caused in my life. Help me to see myself as a place where you can dwell as a precious temple created by you. Thank you for creating me to love you and that you love me. Thank you for cleansing me from the inside out. In Jesus' name I pray. Amen.

Chapter 3
IT'S DARK IN HERE

"But you are a chosen people, a royal priesthood, a holy nation,
God's special possession, that you may declare the praises of him
who called you out of darkness into his wonderful light."
1 Peter 2:9 (NIV)

If you had a looking glass and you could see everything that would result from one decision, would you change your mind? Please let my experience be your looking glass. Look into your future from my past. Let it be a warning of the danger lying ahead so that you can take a different path. Memories get wiped out of our minds when they are too painful to look at. In praying about the abortion I had, I began to realize I couldn't remember a lot surrounding it. I remember the abortion itself; it was traumatic and a living nightmare. But what happened before it? What happened after? I could not remember.

NOT FOR SALE

As I mentioned earlier, my roommate and co-worker asked me if I ever had a one-night stand. It wasn't something that I wanted to do, and I told her no. During this time of my life, I was always being offered something by someone. Satan was trying his best to pull me into a life completely away from God. Be careful when you are not following Christ, and even when you are. People will come to deceive you and pull you into their own way of living. Do I believe they are doing it intentionally? Not always. I believe they are deceived or lost, too. When we are in the world we are drawn to the wrong influences, and they are drawn to us. 2 Corinthians 11:14 says, "Even Satan disguises himself as an angel of light" (NLT). If we are not aware, we can be drawn away.

Not only did my roommate pressure me about one-night stands, but she also introduced me to a man who wanted to "take care of me." He was an older man who wanted to put me into a condo and buy me a car. He said all I had to do was to be there for him whenever he "wanted me." I knew at the very least that I did not want to be bought and captive for this man's pleasure.

I had another woman at another job who wanted me to "live with her son on his yacht." We were at a company lunch at a very expensive restaurant, and she was extremely wealthy. The restaurant overlooked Balboa Park in San Diego. She looked out of the window at the beautiful park as she told me I could have anything I wanted, if I would just agree to live with her son on his yacht. No matter how many times I told her that I had a daughter, she wouldn't stop trying to convince me that they would take care of me.

I didn't know much about the Bible, but I had heard the story of Jesus being tempted by Satan in the desert. She reminded me of Satan in that story, as he told Jesus he could have anything he wanted if He would only bow down and worship him. Matthew 4:8-10, "Again, the devil took him to a very high mountain and showed him all the kingdoms of the world and their splendor. 'All this I will give you,' he said, 'if you will bow down and worship me.' Jesus said to him, 'Away from me, Satan! For it is written: 'Worship the Lord your God, and serve him only'" (NIV). Thankfully, that small amount of biblical knowledge brought enough fear in me to say no to her.

My roommate, however, did talk me into going to dinner with our boss and his guest, a man I did not know. After the dinner in which she drove us to, we went to his guest's house. To my surprise she went into a bedroom with my boss. As she walked into the bedroom with him, she gestured that I should go with his guest. A man who until even today, I do not know; and I did. I followed him into his bedroom. This whole memory was a punch in the stomach to me, not one I wanted to think about.

You see, it hurts even more now because I finally know who I am in Christ. I am worth more than to be used for one night. It hurt like crazy to remember that night. It was like I stepped outside of my body, outside of my own physical mind and watched myself walk into that bedroom. As I remembered I cried and cried, why did I just blindly follow this man into the bedroom? I wanted to just yell, "Don't go in there" and the memory would just go away.

I remember standing in the living room with them the next morning embarrassed, ashamed, and uncomfortable. As we stood there, the man walked into his bedroom and came out with his wallet. He opened it and gave my boss some money. I wanted nothing more than to run out of there. I don't really know what the exchange of money was for; I only know that God brought it to my memory. I've said to myself several times since remembering, maybe he just owed him money for dinner from the night before. I seriously doubt, however, that God triggered my memory with a dinner debt. What hurt so badly is that I just blindly followed this man into his room. I just did what I was told, under the influence of an older woman that I looked up to at the time.

WHAT SATAN MEANT FOR HARM, GOD WILL USE FOR GOOD
I had a "one-night stand." I am not proud of it, and it was buried deep in my shame. I was also promiscuous with others during this time. All of this led to that dark and horrible day of having an abortion. Again, I never blamed other people for my mistakes. I carried each one and blamed myself. I allowed it to weigh me down and cause me to make more mistakes. This one was no exception. Recalling this memory was almost unbearable.

It is at times like these when you must cling to the word of God and His promises. What Satan has meant for harm, God will take it and use it for good if we allow Him. Genesis 50:20 says, "You intended to harm me, but God intended it for good to accomplish what is now being done, the saving of many lives" (NIV). God will use your life and your testimony, what you have been through for His good, to save many lives. God also promises in Job chapter 8:5-7 that our latter days will be greater than our former days. In other words, we have a greater future than our past. "But if you will seek God earnestly and plead with the Almighty, if you are pure and upright, *even now* He will rouse Himself on your behalf and restore you to your prosperous state. Your beginnings will seem humble, so prosperous will your future be" (NIV).

God is waiting "even now" to restore to you all that you've lost. Even now He will "rouse" or "awaken" Himself for you and restore you. Even now, no matter what you've done or what you are doing, He will awaken for you.

ABORTION

"For you created my inmost being;
you knit me together in my mother's womb."
Psalms 139:13 (AMP)

It was after the experience of the one-night stand that I found myself pregnant again. As I said earlier, I was promiscuous during this time. I cannot say it was from this one experience, but it was during this time that I became pregnant again. The influence my roommate/co-worker had over my life was great. She convinced me that I needed to get an abortion, that I could not raise two children on my own. I knew abortion was wrong. I had already given birth to two children. It is a decision that I would regret my whole life, and one only God can heal.

Abortion is the taking of a life. It is *not* a "glob of tissue" as you are told. That is a lie. It is a viable, living creation of God. A Child. A child that is intricately connected not only to your body, but to your soul and to your spirit. When it is removed, you feel its death, you grieve, you suffer, and you have an emptiness in your womb that no one can take away. It is the taking of a life. I felt like a murderer. I wished many times I could be punished. I wanted to go to jail for what I did, for what I saw. It was like a slaughterhouse. I heard the screams of women.

My roommate drove me to the clinic. As we pulled up to the parking lot, I saw people praying. They begged me not to go in. I stopped to talk to them, they said they would help me. They had a van waiting that I could leave in right then. I really wanted to listen to them, I wanted to go with them. I was so confused. My roommate said, "don't listen to them, you can't have another baby!" Instead of listening to them, I listened to her and went into the clinic. I wish to this day I had listened to them.

As I laid on the table in the clinic the abortionist (I cannot call him a doctor; doctors save lives) started to prepare me. Lying there, I thought about the people outside who wanted to help me. I wanted to get in that van and leave with them - I had changed my mind. I told the nurse I didn't want to go through with it. She told the abortionist, "She changed her mind, she wants to stop." He said coldly and irritated, "It's too late, you're already dilated."

I wonder now if what he said was true, if he could have stopped and I could have left. I don't know, but I do know that God is good and faithful. It wasn't until recently that I remembered that I had changed my mind and I tried to leave. God reminded me. These memories get buried so deep that we forget, we choose to forget. Remembering that I had changed my mind didn't change the facts, but it did change the heaviness of the pain and the guilt. Somehow it was eased just a little.

After it was over, I was left alone in the room and I saw my baby. They left it there in a small tray on a table next to me. It was the kind of tray they give you in the hospital to spit in. There was a paper towel over it, covered in blood. I screamed and cried. The nurse came back in. I asked her, "Is that my baby?!" She coldly looked at me and said, "Oh, don't look at *that!*" She picked up my little baby and took it away. I saw tiny little limbs; I saw the blood. It wasn't a *"that,"* it was a baby.

I hated myself. My only comfort is knowing that I will be reunited with my child in Heaven; and the angels have cared for her or him. I will be able to say I'm sorry when I get there. It breaks my heart to know I've missed the beauty of giving life, and that my children have a sibling they have never met. Abortion is a nightmare from the pit of hell and it is a lie. It steals life from the baby and joy from the family.

THE TRUTH ABOUT ABORTION

We are in a different age of truth today than when I had an abortion. Shortly after I had an abortion in the early 1980s pictures of aborted babies began to surface. I joined the pro-life movement and went to many protests. Today you have 3D ultrasounds of life.

You can *see* your baby living inside of you. Yet even with all the technology and social media awareness, many still choose to turn a blind eye. They justify doing wrong because of what they need at the moment, and they call it right.

The Bible clearly warns against this in Isaiah 5:20-21 when it says, "Woe to those who call evil good and good evil, who put darkness for light and light for darkness, who put bitter for sweet and sweet for bitter. Woe to those who are wise in their own eyes and clever in their own sight" (NIV). And as we continue to turn away from what we do not want to admit, God warns us in the book of Hebrews that our hearts can become hardened to the truth. Hebrews 3:7, "So, as the Holy Spirit says: "Today, if you hear his voice, do not harden your hearts" (NIV).

The truth is that abortion takes a human life for the sake of convenience, or inconvenience, out of fear or uncertainty. Those who are performing the abortion do not use the technology available and offer a look at the baby. They have stuck to the same story since I had an abortion more than 30 years ago. "It is a blob of tissue, not a viable human being." "A clump of cells." "It is over quickly."

What they do not tell you is that you will suffer a lifetime of regret, and it will take a lot of work to overcome losing a child. I know there are many who might even be reading this right now saying, "I had an abortion and I have no regret." But dare I say if not here on earth, someday we will all (myself included) answer before God for our actions, and that will include abortion.

MISSING GENERATIONS

Jeremiah 1:5 says, "Before I formed you in the womb I knew you, before you were born I set you apart; I appointed you as a prophet to the nations" (NIV). God knew us before we were even conceived. He knew our names, hair color, eye color, the shape of our faces. He knew everything about us, he knit us together in our mothers' wombs. He had a plan for us before we were born. He appointed us prophets, kings, doctors, lawyers, presidents, congressmen and women, artists, musicians, writers, actors, fishermen, scuba divers, surfers, restaurant owners, businesspeople, pastors, priests, husbands, wives, and on and on. Generations have been wiped out by abortion.

The National Right to Life Committee indicated there have been an estimated 63,459,781 abortions since the Supreme Court handed down its 1973 Roe vs. Wade decision allowing virtually unlimited abortions.[1] Our world has missed out on the gifts and talents of over sixty-three million human beings because of it; over *sixty-three million.* I have often thought that we need a visual of the number of lives lost. What if we had over sixty-three million pairs of baby shoes in one place? How big of a field would we need to place them in?

Psalms 139:13-16 says, "For you created my inmost being; you knit me together in my mother's womb. I praise you because I am fearfully and wonderfully made; your works are wonderful, I know that full well. My frame was not hidden from you when I was made in the secret place, when I was woven together in the depths of the earth. Your eyes saw my unformed body; all the days ordained for me were written in your book before one of them came to be" (NIV). What strikes me most about this scripture is *all the days ordained for me were written in your book before one of them came to be.* Plans were written down by God before one of them came to be. How it must grieve God's heart when He knows the good plans He has for each child that is not allowed to be born at our hands.

CHOOSE LIFE

I follow a lot of the newer pro-life groups on social media. By newer I mean younger, college student pro-life groups. I'm interested to see what younger people are facing. I not only have a son in college, but grandchildren. I see the climate of hostility and it is disheartening.

I know many people who might read this may come out against me as they do these groups on social media. I see the arguments, "It's not your body, it's mine," "Leave my body alone," "You don't care for the mother carrying the baby, you just care for the clump of cells who is not a human"; and many other statements. I see what I am in for, and it's okay. In order to keep justifying ourselves, we have to allow our hearts to become hardened to the truth.

What does this mean in the word of God? Acts 28:27 says, "For this people's heart has become calloused; they hardly hear with their ears, and they have closed their eyes. Otherwise they might see with their eyes, hear with their ears, understand with their hearts and turn, and I would heal them" (NIV). This is a powerful statement and scripture to a society today who "hardly hear with their ears" and have "closed their eyes." In other words, we are closing our eyes and turning away from the truth. Yes, it is true that the baby is growing inside the woman's body, and her body is her own. But the baby is a human life. The baby has its own DNA separate from its mother's DNA. Each one of us are individuals created by God.

As I said earlier, with the technology available today and all of the information on how abortions are performed, we simply are closing our eyes and turning away from the truth. I had the honor of going to many of my daughter's recent ultrasounds, and most magnificently a 3D ultrasound of my granddaughter. It was amazing to get a glimpse of the life growing within her; from the first sign of a heartbeat to seeing her actual face, hands, and feet.

We saw her smile, could see her eyelashes, and she even grimaced when the technician moved her around. It was the most amazing thing I have ever seen. She was beautiful. She was playing with her hair inside of my daughter's womb; and to this day she plays with her hair when she goes to sleep. She is now three years old and when I look into her beautiful blue eyes, I am so thankful she is here. When I held her as a newborn baby I could not help thinking of the babies who did not have the same opportunity to live. It breaks my heart, but more importantly it breaks God's heart.

In this book I have talked a lot about the mistakes I have made in life, but I have also done a lot of things right. I am the proudest of my children. I have raised some amazing children who are now adults and have given me beautiful grandchildren. My children have brought me laughter and joy and my life would not be the same without them. It doesn't matter how your children were conceived, in love or not, they are still a promise and a gift from God. They are innocent and blameless and have nothing to do with how they were conceived; and they deserve life. I do not regret and will never regret having my children. They are and have been a blessing to me and in many ways, they saved my life. What I do regret is the abortion. It is not too late to open our eyes and see the truth. Please do it, before it's too late. Choose life.

HEALING FROM ABORTION

"Praise the Lord, my soul, and forget not all his benefits- who forgives all your sins and heals all your diseases, who redeems your life from the pit and crowns you with love and compassion, who satisfies your desires with good things so that your youth is renewed like the eagle's."
Psalms 103:2-5 (NIV)

If you have had an abortion God will forgive you, just as He has forgiven me. You cannot carry the burden of an abortion; you have to lay it at the cross of Jesus. You have to know that He forgives you, and that you can receive healing and move on. If you need to, seek the help you need through your church or through the many organizations you can find online who offer support and counseling. Make sure that you find a group who offers prayer. Most of all, know that you are forgiven.

GO AND SIN NO MORE

Know that Jesus is the kindest friend that you will ever have. When the woman caught in adultery was thrown at the feet of Jesus by her

Know that

Jesus

is the

kindest friend

you will

ever have.

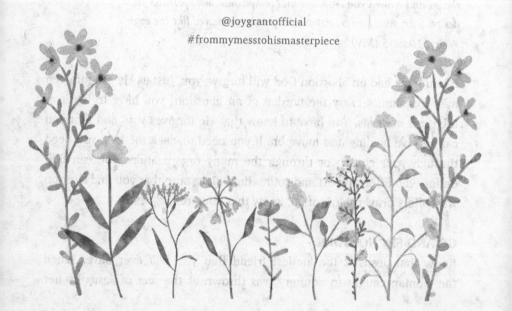

accusers, Jesus had compassion on her. John 8:1-11, "Jesus returned to the Mount of Olives, but early the next morning he was back again at the Temple. A crowd soon gathered, and he sat down and taught them. As he was speaking, the teachers of religious law and the Pharisees brought a woman who had been caught in the act of adultery. They put her in front of the crowd.

'Teacher,' they said to Jesus, 'this woman was caught in the act of adultery. The law of Moses says to stone her. What do you say?'

They were trying to trap Him into saying something they could use against him, but Jesus stooped down and wrote in the dust with his finger. They kept demanding an answer, so He stood up again and said, 'All right, but let the one who has never sinned throw the first stone!' Then He stooped down again and wrote in the dust.

When the accusers heard this, they slipped away one by one, beginning with the oldest, until only Jesus was left in the middle of the crowd with the woman. Then Jesus stood up again and said to the woman, 'Where are your accusers? Didn't even one of them condemn you?' 'No, Lord,' she said. And Jesus said, 'Neither do I. Go and sin no more'" (NLT).

In this story the Pharisees were trying to trap Jesus with a "trick question." The law said a woman caught in adultery must be stoned. The Pharisees did not care about the lost condition of the woman, but Jesus did. He had compassion on her. Jesus *was the only one who had no sin.* He was the *only one who could have thrown the first stone,* but He didn't. Instead, He sent away her accusers and was left alone with only her. He had compassion on her, and He has compassion on you. Your sin condemns you, but Jesus does not. Jesus sends your accusers away and says, "Neither do I condemn you. Go and sin no more."

Isaiah 1:18 9 says, "Come now, and let us reason together," saith the Lord. "Though your sins be as scarlet, they shall be as white as snow; though they be red like crimson, they shall be as wool" (KJV). It is good to know that though our sins are as scarlet, Jesus comes to us and washes us as white as snow. When you come to Him and ask Him to forgive you, not only does He forgive you, but He cleanses you from the past. He gives you a new life, a new start. You need only ask and receive it. Believe it, and it is yours. Though you remember the pain, He forgives, and He forgets. He will begin to heal you and strengthen you as you begin to ask.

So, whatever it is that you are suffering from right now as you read, whether it is having had an abortion, maybe multiple abortions; whatever it is that is weighing you down and condemning you in your soul, know that *Jesus Himself does not condemn you.* There is nothing that He will not and does not forgive. Whatever it is that is causing you to fall, be it sex, drugs, anger, alcohol, infidelity, love of money, greed; whatever it is, lay it down. Ask God for forgiveness and receive it. Seek Him for the grace and the strength to "go and sin no more."

Chapter 3

STUDY GUIDE

REFLECT Can you face some of your worst memories and trust Jesus to guide you through them?

Name one memory that you need to lay at the feet of Jesus.

There are not only Godly influences around us; but also dark and deceiving influences. What are some of the negative influences that you can eliminate from your life?

What are some of the positive influences that you can embrace more of in your life?

READ John 8:7-11 "But Jesus bent down and started to write on the ground with his finger. When they kept on questioning him, he straightened up and said to them, 'Let any one of you who is without sin be the first to throw a stone at her.' Again he stooped down and wrote on the ground. At this, those who heard began to go away one at a time, the older ones first, until only Jesus was left, with the woman still standing there. Jesus straightened up and asked her, 'Woman, where are they? Has no one condemned you?' 'No one, sir,' she said. 'Then neither do I condemn you,' Jesus declared. 'Go now and leave your life of sin.'"

Job 8:5-7 "But if you will seek God earnestly and plead with the Almighty, if you are pure and upright, even now He will rouse Himself on your behalf and restore you to your prosperous state. Your beginnings will seem humble, so prosperous will your future be."

Isaiah 1:18 "Come now, and let us reason together," saith the Lord. "Though your sins be as scarlet, they shall be as white as snow; though they be red like crimson, they shall be as wool."

Psalms 103:2-5 "Praise the Lord, my soul, and forget not all his benefits- who forgives all your sins and heals all your diseases, who redeems your life from the pit and crowns you with love and compassion, who satisfies your desires with good things so that your youth is renewed like the eagle's."

DECLARE There is nothing that I have done or that I will do that God does not already know about. There are no secrets with an Almighty Father. I only need to humble myself and go to Him as His child and ask for His forgiveness and His strength to move forward. He is there with open arms waiting to forgive me and to help me. I will trust Him!

PRAY Father, please bring to my mind any negative influences that I am allowing into my life. Please give me the courage and the strength to walk away from them and to follow You. Please heal me of my deepest wounds and of my worst memories. Help me to forgive those who have hurt me; and most of all, help me to forgive myself just as You have forgiven me. In Jesus' name I pray. Amen.

Chapter 4
A PROMISE TO BE GOOD

"By myself I can do nothing..."
John 5:30 (NIV)

After the abortion, I moved from California to Georgia to be close to my family. However, there is one memory from before the move that I think is important to mention. I only remembered this recently. I was working for a government contractor. Passing through security each day I would see a very attractive guy, a California Highway Patrolman (CHIP) who would flirt with me. I was so excited when he asked me to dinner. I met him at an Italian restaurant looking beautiful, but this turned into just another opportunity for someone to take advantage of me. Why did I attract these types? Was it my own insecurity, or was I just vulnerable? We sat at dinner chatting, and the more we chatted, the more wine he ordered for me to drink. I believe the waiter was the owner of the restaurant. He was a fatherly type and looked so concerned for me. He kept asking me to order dinner. I also remember the look of disapproval he gave to my date. I got the impression he was a regular there.

We did finally order dinner, but I don't remember eating it. The next thing I remember is waking up naked in this man's bed and needing to throw up. I was so upset, embarrassed and ashamed as I sat on a stranger's bathroom floor naked and sick. I got dressed and went outside not knowing where I was. My car was not there. He must have driven me there as I passed out. I woke him to take me to my car. When I moved to Georgia, I felt the need to apologize to this man. I wrote him a letter saying that was not the type of girl I was or wanted to be. Why did I feel the need to do this? Instead of a letter, I should have been filing sexual assault charges, but my shame was overwhelming to the point of blaming myself once again.

Once in Georgia, I got a job and worked as a single mom to raise my daughter. I was in my early 20s, still going out with friends, searching to find my way. I spent a lot of time with my mother and father. We never talked about the past. My father seemed happier, more content and at ease. Maybe something in his older age and being able to retire changed him or maybe I had just grown up. I could visit and go back to my place; it made it easier that I didn't have to live with him. It didn't bother me to sit and watch television anymore, I actually enjoyed it. I felt very dedicated to them.

I didn't have to, but I brought my father part of my salary every paycheck. I wanted to help them. I was thankful for them, but I had a displaced need to take care of them. When I was only 17 years old, I had the chance to live with family in New York, to finish high school, and go to college. But when I called my parents in Illinois to ask for permission, I was met with fury from my father and tears from my mother. She begged me to come back asking, "who will protect me from your father?" I felt the burden and worry to take care of her, so I went back and gave up a life changing opportunity. The need to "protect" my mom carried through my life until she passed in 2018. I loved her very much; and in the end, I was determined to see her happy and enjoy her final years.

By the time I was 23, my father was diagnosed with lung cancer. I helped my mother care for him until he passed away in hospice. The sickness humbled him, and I saw a glimpse of Jesus in him before he died. One day he hugged me in the kitchen. He was crying and asked me to forgive him for the past. There was a small amount of healing in that moment that I will never forget. I had the opportunity to talk with him and somehow even though I was still lost, I made sure he knew Jesus before he died.

AN OFFICE BET

I had not been with anyone since the abortion. I dated someone for a short period of time, and as usual, he dumped me when I would not sleep with him. Then my dad died. Satan always knows when you are the most vulnerable. I finally had some sort of relationship with my father, and he was gone. I was hurting from the death of my father, and I began looking for the wrong comfort again. I began to see someone I worked with, and I began to sleep with him. I really liked him and, of course, like the others I hoped for more; but how could I hope for more as I continued in the same pattern of giving myself away.

By 24 I found myself pregnant again. I had flown to California for my job and knowing I was pregnant once again, prayed to God in my hotel room. I found a Bible in the drawer of my room, opened it, and immediately saw this verse: Deuteronomy 30:19, "This day I call the heavens and the earth as witnesses against you that I have set before you life and death, blessings and curses. Now choose life, so that you and your children may live" (NIV).

It was on this trip with my job that I found out from a mutual friend that the guy I was dating, the father of this child, saw me as nothing more than an office bet. He had bet a few friends that he could get me to sleep with him, I guess he won that bet. Despite finding out this sad news I knew there was no way I would lose this baby again to abortion; especially after God led me to that scripture. I never read the Bible then and I didn't carry one with me; so, it was no coincidence that God put that scripture in front of me. The word of God is an amazing book. Nothing surprises God, not even abortion. His word is alive and breathing. How else can you open the Bible and find scriptures that pertain to life *before* being formed in the womb and *choosing life* not death. Nothing you do surprises God, it may break His heart, but He is always there waiting to forgive and heal you. Any question you have in life you can find the answer to in the Bible, even abortion.

After I lost my son to adoption, I was secretly happy when I got pregnant with my daughter at 18. I would have a baby to hold again. Now, again after the trauma of an abortion, I was secretly happy to have another chance at life with this child. I was still conforming to a pattern of the world that Romans 12:2 talks about.

Afraid of being pregnant and alone again, I knew I had to change, but I didn't know how. One night as I was driving to pick up my daughter after work I found myself crying out to God for help. I pulled over on the side of the road. I got out of the car and fell to my knees in the dark. I can still remember how the gravel on the road felt on my knees. I asked God to forgive me, and I made a promise to Him "to be good." Just like the 14-year-old girl sitting on her bedroom floor, I wanted to be good and promised to be good.

The problem was I made that commitment to God in my own strength. I did not know how to seek God for *His* goodness and *His* strength. We can try to be good on our own, but when it comes to something as deep as buried wounds of the past or addiction, in most cases we will fail. In John 6:63 Jesus said, "It is the Spirit who gives life; the flesh is no help at all. The words that I have spoken to you are spirit and life" (ESV). We need the power of God's Holy Spirit that enables us and gives us the strength to change and resist temptation. Our "flesh" or trying to change in our own strength will fail us. We will eventually run out of strength.

JESUS OUR HEALER

I had my second daughter at just 28 ½ weeks into the pregnancy. She was exactly 3 lbs. Her lungs were underdeveloped, and she became very ill and nearly died. God saved her life; she was a miracle baby. Other than that night on the side of the road, this was the first time I prayed. I mean really prayed. I didn't have a close relationship with Christ, but I knew He was the only one who could save my daughter. I stayed by her side the night the doctor told me she would not make it through the night. I stayed and

I prayed. A priest came to see me while I was with her and said he was sent to pray because my daughter was going to die. An anger rose in me that I had never experienced before and I said, "She is not going to die! If you are going to pray anything, pray that God heals her otherwise do not touch my baby!" He pulled out a vial of oil and anointed her head and prayed for God's healing. The next morning, to the doctor's amazement her lungs were healed, and she would recover.

In Matthew 8:5-13 a Roman Centurion came to Jesus seeking healing for one of his servants. Being a Roman he was not a follower of Jesus, but he had heard of Jesus who heals. "When Jesus had entered Capernaum, a centurion came to Him asking for help. 'Lord,' he said, 'my servant lies at home paralyzed, suffering terribly.' Jesus said to him, 'Shall I come and heal him. The centurion replied, 'Lord, I do not deserve to have you come under my roof. But just say the word, and my servant will be healed. For I myself am a man under authority, with soldiers under me. I tell this one, 'Go,' and he goes; and that one, 'Come,' and he comes. I say to my servant, 'Do this,' and he does it,' and will. When Jesus heard this, he was amazed and said to those following him, 'Truly I tell you, I have not found anyone in Israel with such great faith...' Then Jesus said to the centurion, 'Go! Let it be done just as you believed it would.' And his servant was healed at that moment" (NIV).

MY DAUGHTER

My daughter was healed in one night. She weighed less than a pound and a half by then. Both of her lungs were completely collapsed, machines were breathing for her tiny body and tubes bigger than her extended out. She was covered in wires, beeps, machines, sounds, she had been poked so many times that they ran out of tiny veins and had lines in her tiny head. I was amazed at how small she was. She should have still been in my womb, growing and safe.

Instead, she was fighting to live, her little hand as big as the tip of my finger. I stared at her in awe and looked around the Neonatal Intensive Care Unit at all of the tiny, fighting babies. I watched as the many staff and doctors attended to each baby with intensity, including mine. Then reality hit me. There in that room, in that hospital they were fighting to save these tiny premature babies; but across town in abortion clinics, they were taking their tiny lives. The irony and reality were overwhelming.

God sees life and that night He chose to heal my daughter. Today she is healthy, whole, married and with her first child. I will never forget the glow on the doctor's face when he came in with the x-rays of her lungs, amazed that they were clear. It was God. No one else could have done that. He heard my prayer. So, if you are sitting reading this now, believe for whatever miracle you need.

I was not a great Christian praying at my daughter's bedside. Like the centurion, I was not even following Jesus. I only prayed by the roadside, and then that night. I was only a mother who believed. God is no respecter of persons; He hears your cries. He will answer your prayers. You do not have to be a pastor or a great leader of God to believe that God will heal you or your loved ones. You need only to believe with your whole heart. God listens, He hears, and He answers.

TIRED OF WAITING

"But they that wait upon the Lord shall renew their strength"
Isaiah 40:31 (KJV)

After having my second daughter I began counting the days, weeks, months, and then the years of "being good." To me, being good meant staying out of a relationship and not having sex. I was determined to keep my commitment to God that I made that night on the side of the road. The longer I would go, the more I thought God was proud of me. For eleven years, I never slept with another man. During that time, I learned to pray and went to church faithfully. I raised both of my daughters in a spirit filled church; and worked hard through prayer and counseling to forgive my father.

Life was far from perfect. I was still a single mom working full time, but I was learning to lean on God. I used to open the windows and pray to the north, south, east and the west. I prophesied and was prophesied over. I was hungry for God and for His word. I read my Bible from cover to cover until it literally fell apart. But even though I *felt good* *"being good,"* I was still relying on my own personal strength. I really thought I had made it until I hit that wall where my strength ran out and loneliness hit.

I was in love with God and wanted to experience all He had for me; but I began to look at young couples at church and I was alone. They looked so happy together with their children. Now in my 30s and a single parent, I compared my situation to theirs and the loneliness grew deeper and stronger. I longed to be married and to know what it was like to be loved and cared for. My three sisters were married, had homes and husbands; they stayed at home to raise their children. I was still single, working full time, struggling and alone; what was wrong with me? I became tired of waiting on God. Isaiah 40:30 says, "Even youths grow tired and weary, and young men stumble and fall..." (NIV). I became weary and was about to stumble badly. Not only did God see my loneliness, but the enemy saw it and seized the opportunity to step in. That is when I met my now ex-husband. Everything about the situation and relationship with him was wrong.

SELFISHNESS

I was involved in church at the time and interested in someone who was in the choir with me; but the voices in my head said that a Christian man would never be interested in me. It was the voice of the liar, the enemy. John 8:44 says speaking of the devil that is Satan, "He was a murderer from the beginning, and does not stand in the truth, because there is no truth in him. When he lies, he speaks out of his own character, for he is a liar and the father of lies" (ESV). I did not recognize the voice of the enemy at the time. Had I recognized it, I could have resisted it. If I understood who I was in Christ, I would not have known not to listen to that voice.

Instead, I believed these thoughts were my own. Zechariah 3:1 says of Satan, "Then the angel showed me Joshua the high priest standing before the Angel of the LORD, with Satan standing at his right hand to *accuse him*" (NIV). Satan accused and condemned, telling me that I was not good enough for a Christian man in church by saying, "Look at your past, you have children out of wedlock, don't even try. You'll never be good enough for someone like him. He'll never be interested in you." Even though I was young and attractive, going to church, had a good job, drove a nice car, none of those things mattered. Those were outward things, but the inward was still broken. Still not understanding my worth in Christ, I believed the lies. I accepted less because I believed I *deserved* less.

I had to purposely become rebellious against God to date my ex-husband. I threw away everything I had held out hope for those eleven years. I pushed aside my morals, my good judgement, and even my own daughter who was my priority in life. I became selfish. I did not recognize or like myself. I wanted love, I wanted a relationship, and I was tired of waiting. I was telling God, "I know better than you and I am going to do this my way." When we stop waiting on God and do things our way there is a price to pay. A price paid not only by us, but by those who are affected around us.

TAKING MATTERS INTO YOUR OWN HANDS

In the book of Genesis Abraham and Sarah did just this. They did not wait on God for the son that was promised to them; instead, they took matters into their own hands. In Genesis Chapter 12 God began to promise Abraham at the age of 75 that he would be a father to many descendants (a great nation). His wife Sarah was unable to bear children and was 65 years old. I am sure that they had tried all of their marriage to have children. I can imagine their excitement at hearing from God; their dreams of having a child were finally coming true. But ten years passed by, and nothing happened. Ten years of waiting and believing God for their miracle, a son. Despite the constant promises from God to Abraham (called Abram at the time) in Genesis chapters 12 through 15, Sarah (called Sarai at the time) took matters into her own hands.

CREATING OUR OWN PROBLEMS

In Genesis Chapter 16, tired of waiting and frustrated, Sarai decided that her maidservant, Hagar, could possibly be the way that they would have a child. I am sure she heard the "voices in her head" telling her, "Don't wait on God anymore! You can do this yourself." (By now I hope you can recognize whose voice this is. The voice of the liar, the enemy.) She told her husband, Abram, to take her maidservant, Hagar, and get her pregnant to bear them a child. Abram, too, must have toiled with this idea, and then gave into the "voices" that said, "do it." Abram then had a son with Hagar, and his name was Ishmael. Abram was 86 years old when Ishmael was born, Sarai was 76.

The birth of Ishmael did not solve their problems, it only added to them. Hagar resented Sarai, perhaps for making her bear a child for her; or maybe because she wanted to be Abram's wife. Maybe both. I'm sure Hagar was much younger, more beautiful and of childbearing age. Although the Bible does talk about Sarai's beauty even at her age, she was barren. Enmity was arising between them both. Hagar had the child; Sarai had the husband. What a bad idea, why didn't they just wait on God. The resentment between them grew and the Bible says that Sarai dealt harshly with Hagar and demanded that Abram send her away:

Genesis 16:1-6, "Now Sarai, Abram's wife, had not been able to bear children for him. But she had an Egyptian servant named Hagar. So, Sarai said to Abram, 'The LORD has prevented me from having children.'" (Notice she is blaming God instead of believing His promises.) "'Go and sleep with my servant. Perhaps I can have children through her.' And Abram agreed with Sarai's proposal. So, Sarai, Abram's wife, took Hagar the Egyptian servant and gave her to Abram as a wife" (This happened ten years after Abram had settled in the land of Canaan. Ten years after the promise of a child.) "So Abram had sexual relations with Hagar, and she became pregnant. But when Hagar knew she was pregnant, she began to treat her mistress, Sarai, with contempt. Then Sarai said to Abram, 'This is all your fault! I put my servant into your arms, but now that she's pregnant she treats me with contempt. The LORD will show who's wrong—you or me!'" (Now she's

blaming her husband for their mistake!) "Abram replied, 'Look, she is your
servant, so deal with her as you see fit.' Then Sarai treated Hagar so harshly
that she finally ran away" (NLT).

God, however, is faithful and kind. He heard Hagar's cries, came to
her, and blessed her. He told her to go back; and not only would she be
protected, but she would also be blessed, Genesis 16:7-10, "The angel of
the LORD found Hagar beside a spring of water in the wilderness, along
the road to Shur. The angel said to her, 'Hagar, Sarai's servant, where
have you come from, and where are you going?' 'I'm running away from
my mistress, Sarai,' she replied. The angel of the LORD said to her, 'Return
to your mistress, and submit to her authority.' Then he added, 'I will give
you more descendants than you can count'" (NLT).

So, Hagar returned and gave birth to her son, Ishmael, and Abram
was eighty-six years old at the time of his birth. Between the chapters
of Genesis 16 & 17 it seems God is silent. This must have been a time
of growing and reflecting for them. Ishmael is now 13, Abram is 99 and
Sarai is 89. After thirteen years, God begins to speak to Abram again
about having a son; an heir; a son that will be given to him and Sarai.
God changes Abram's name to Abraham, meaning Father of Nations; and
changes Sarai's name to Sarah, Mother of Nations. It wasn't because God
did not love Ishmael, God promised to bless Ishmael; but Ishmael was not
born of Abraham and Sarah as God had promised.

NOT BELIEVING THE PROMISES OF GOD
God begins to appear again to Abraham and speaks His covenant to him;
promising him that nations will come forth from him; and an inheritance
of the land of Canaan, now Israel. Perhaps since it has been so long since
Abraham has heard from God that he forgot God's promises and speaks to
God about Ishmael. Not only that Abraham laughs and doubts God.

Genesis 17:17-18, "Then Abraham bowed down to the ground,
but he laughed to himself in disbelief. 'How could I become a father at
the age of 100?' he thought. 'And how can Sarah have a baby when she
is ninety years old?' So, Abraham said to God, 'May Ishmael live under

your special blessing!'" (NLT). But God corrects him time and time again that His promises will come through blessing his wife Sarah with a child. Genesis 17:19, "But God said, 'No, Sarah your wife shall bear you a son indeed, and you shall name him Isaac (laughter); and I will establish My covenant with him for an everlasting covenant and with his descendants after him'" (AMP).

Soon after this the Lord appears to Abraham again, this time in the form of a man (who is thought to be Jesus) with two angels. Then the promise of a son comes again to Abraham through this visit telling him that by this time next year, Sarah will bare him a son. Sarah who was nearby listening, laughed in disbelief because of her old age (maybe this is why God said Isaac's name would mean "laughter"). Genesis 18:13-14, "And the Lord said to Abraham, 'Why did Sarah laugh, saying, 'Shall I surely bear *a child,* since I am old?' Is anything too hard for the Lord? At the appointed time I will return to you, according to the time of life, and Sarah shall have a son'" (NKJV).

God's promises are faithful and true, despite Abraham and Sarah's doubts and laughter, God fulfills His promise exactly one year later in Genesis 21:1-3, "The Lord graciously remembered and visited Sarah as He had said, and the Lord did for her as He had promised. So, Sarah conceived and gave birth to a son for Abraham in his old age, at the appointed time of which God had spoken to him. Abraham named his son Isaac (laughter), the son to whom Sarah gave birth" (AMP). Abraham was 100 years old and Sarah 90, when Isaac was born.

WAITING ON GOD

But soon jealousy and enmity would rise again; but this time between Ishmael and Isaac, and once again Hagar is sent away with her son. Genesis 21:9-11, "Now [as time went on] Sarah saw [Ishmael] the son of Hagar the Egyptian, whom she had borne to Abraham, mocking [Isaac]. Therefore, she said to Abraham, 'Drive out this maid and her son, for the son of this maid shall not be an heir with my son Isaac.' The situation distressed Abraham greatly because of his son [Ishmael]" (AMP). Sarah sent them out from their land but God kept His promise and blessed Ishmael with his own land and nations.

What if Abraham and Sarah had just waited on God? Could it have been that God was going to bring forth Isaac in the 11th year or 12th year after his first promise to Abraham? How would it have changed history and the course of time had they just waited? But even though they did not wait, God still had a plan for their lives despite their doubt and unbelief. He still blessed Ishmael, and He brought forth His promise of a son to Sarah and Abraham. How much pain could have been avoided if they had just waited. How many lives and generations were affected?

It was 25 years from the time that Abraham was promised a son until Isaac was born. In between those 25 years he messed up probably more than we know. He offered his wife three times to kings to save his own skin, saying a "white lie" that she was his sister. He slept with Hagar and did not wait on God. He could have said no to Sarah, but he gave into the temptation. They had to deal not only with the consequences of impatience with God, but with generations of pain. But because of God's great love and mercy, He fulfilled His promises and covenants with Abraham. God could have said, "I'll find someone else to bless," but He didn't. God waited, God let Abraham fall, and then God picked him up again.

Abraham could not undo having Ishmael, but he could still believe God for Isaac. We cannot change what we have done in the past, but we can believe in God to change our future. We can hold onto the promises that God gives us and look forward to change. We can avoid future pain if we listen to Him and wait on Him. Not only can we avoid pain for ourselves but pain for those around us and for generations to come. It isn't too late. It wasn't too late for Abraham at 100 and Sarah at 90 years old. God looked at them and said, "I made a promise to you, and I will keep it."

Ishmael and Isaac had the same father, Abraham; but most importantly, they had God the Father. An angel of the Lord appeared to Hagar and encouraged her, and she was given promises from God for her son. Hagar had a choice to raise her son in the promises of God, just as

Abraham and Sarah did. We don't know whether she did or not, but we do know that in Genesis 16:12 God saw Ishmael's rebellion even before he was born saying to Hagar, "This son of yours will be a wild man, as untamed as a wild donkey! He will raise his fist against everyone, and everyone will be against him. Yes, he will live in open hostility against all his relatives" (NLT). Even though God saw Ishmael's future decisions, He still said He would bless him, and He did. God does not break His promises to us.

WHEN WE ARE TIRED, WE NEED TO TRUST

We all have choices to make. Ishmael's rebellion was not Abraham's fault, nor was it Hagar's fault. His decisions to rebel remained with himself, just as ours do. Of course, his past hurt affected his decisions, but it didn't change the fact that he had a choice to do good or not to do good; to have peace with his brothers or not to have peace. This is where our decisions and our responsibilities for our own actions lie. They lie with our ability to forgive those who hurt us, and to find peace with God in our lives for our future and for generations to come. When we are tired of waiting on God and trying on our own, these are the times we need to seek God with all of our heart and trust Him. Proverbs 3:5-6 says, "*Trust in the Lord with all your heart, and lean not on your own understanding; In all your ways acknowledge Him, and He shall direct your paths*" (NKJV).

What is it that you are waiting on God for? Does it seem that He is being silent with you as it was with Abraham the 13 years between Ishmael's birth and conceiving Isaac? Has he made promises to you that you do not believe, perhaps you are laughing at God as Abraham and Sarah did? Did you take matters into your own hands and feel you have messed up so bad there is no other chance? What is He promising you today? Don't walk away from Him anymore. Generations can be affected. He wants to bless you, your children, and your grandchildren right now. It is never too late.

Habakkuk 2:3 says, "For the vision is yet for an appointed time, but at the end it shall speak, and not lie: though it tarry, wait for it;

because it will surely come, it will not tarry" (NKJV). Trust Him and wait on Him, your promises surely will come to pass.

MY GOODNESS IS NOTHING APART FROM YOU, GOD

"O my soul, you have said to the Lord, You are my Lord,
My goodness is nothing apart from You."
Psalms 16:2 (NKJV)

God is loving, God is patient; but this time I believe God had to lift His hand of protection from me because I knew better. I had to turn my back on God and His teachings to be with my ex-husband. I knew that I should wait for marriage to have sex. I knew that I should be dated, courted, treated well, and loved. This time I allowed myself to believe what I knew was not true; that he did love me, he did want a relationship with me, and would marry me. He had a daughter younger than mine. He seemed like a good single father, but it would not take long for the truth to come through.

Wanting so badly to know what it was like to be married, I allowed myself to be blinded by my desires. Just as Sarah pushed Abraham to sin, I fell into a place of sin that would cost us dearly. God was warning me, but I ignored the signs. I was willing to push aside what God had taught me: to wait upon Him. Even in trying to be good on my own, I was drawing closer to God; but I became lost in the hope of being loved and of having what others had. I became focused on what I did not have and longed to fulfill my desires. Romans 8:5 says, "Those who live according to the flesh have their minds set on what the flesh desires; but those who live in accordance with the Spirit have their minds set on what the Spirit desires" (NIV). Sarah had her mind set on having a child and brought Hagar into their lives. I had my mind set on my fleshly desires to be married and loved. Blessings are delayed through disobedience. God didn't remove the promise of a child from Abraham and Sarah, but it became delayed.

Were the things I desired bad? Was Sarah's desire for a child bad? Not at all. But God wanted to fulfill those desires for her and for me. Just

When we are
tired of "waiting,"
these are the
times we need to
seek God with
all of our heart
and trust Him.

like Sarah, I did not want to wait any more. In my impatience I allowed myself to go down a path that I knew was wrong. A path that could have led to my and my children's total destruction. Just as Romans 8:6 goes on to say, "The mind governed by the flesh is death, but the mind governed by the Spirit is life and peace" (NIV). I forfeited life and peace for the desires of my flesh.

LONELINESS

Proverbs 23:7 says, "For as he thinks in his heart, so is he" (NKJV). The Bible applies to everyone, so you can also insert as "she" thinks in "her" heart, so is "she." I dwelled on my loneliness, and it entered my heart. I then allowed myself to act on that loneliness.

I became "governed by my flesh" and it could have led to not only emotional death, but even physical death in an emotionally abusive relationship. When I met my ex-husband, God began to show me the signs, the red warning flags, but I ignored them. My heart then started to become hard to the word of God so that I could do what I wanted to do. Romans 8:7-8, "The mind governed by the flesh is *hostile to God; it does not submit to God's law, nor can it do so.* Those who are in the realm of the flesh cannot please God" (NIV).

Not only did I put my relationship with my daughter, who was still at home with me, in danger; I put my relationship with God in danger. Instead of finding the good things I had hoped for, I found disaster. God *always* has our best in mind when He warns us. He sees the road ahead of us that we choose to ignore.

CHOOSING TO BE BLIND

Romans 7:19, "I want to do what is good, but I don't. I don't want to do what is wrong, but I do it anyway" (NLT). This is what focusing on our fleshly desires does. It causes us to do the very thing that we do not want to do. We repeat our mistakes. We choose to do wrong.

I chose to be blind to fulfill my own needs. I hold myself more responsible than I do my ex-husband. I was a Christian, and he was not.

I knew better and I had the responsibility of being an example to him. I believe that if I had done things God's way, God would have either worked in the relationship with him; or kept me from heartache. Instead, I got tired of waiting and did what I wanted.

This is what God says about this in 2 Peter 2:21-22, "It would have been better for them not to have known the way of righteousness, than to have known it and then to turn their backs on the sacred command that was passed on to them. Of them the proverbs are true: 'A dog returns to its vomit,' and, 'A sow that is washed returns to her wallowing in the mud'" (NIV). The proverb spoken of in this scripture is Proverbs 26:11, "Like a dog that returns to his vomit is a fool who repeats his foolishness" (NASB). God says it would be better that I *did not know the way of righteousness* than to have *known it and turned back*. That is what I did, I knew it and I turned back. Now like the dog returning to its vomit, I was a fool returning to my ways instead of waiting on God. Even worse, a washed clean sow returning to wallow in the mud. In other words, washed clean by the blood of Jesus, and returning to the sin. Ouch, that stings.

HIS LOVE IS FREE

Our salvation is not a guarantee that doing the right thing will come easily. Our walk with God is just that, a walk. It is a journey and an effort to get to know Him and His word. His word strengthens us, and He speaks to us through it. He guides, teaches and protects us with His word. You cannot be "good" on your own. You can try, I did it for eleven years, but eventually your human strength will run out. Psalms 16:1-2 says, "Preserve me, O God, for in You I put my *Trust*. O my soul, you have said to the Lord, You are my Lord, my goodness is nothing apart from You" (NKJV). Counting the days, months and years of not having a relationship with a man did not change how God felt about me. It only changed how I felt about *myself*. I thought that the longer I waited, the prouder God was of me. I was trying to earn His love and His approval to make up for my past.

What I did not understand was that God *already loved me* and was *already proud of me*. God *loves you* and *is proud of you*. You cannot earn

61

His love. You already have it. Jesus paid for it, and it is free to receive. If I was as confident in His love then as I am now, I would not have compared myself to other people and what they had. I would not have looked so strongly at what I *didn't have*. Sure, I get lonely now, but I don't let it control me. I don't let it drive my life. I won't allow it to take me down the wrong path like I allowed it then. You have to know that Jesus paid it ALL for you on the cross and that He loves you. He can fulfill every need of loneliness and longing that you have.

Isaiah 54:5 says, "For your husband is your Maker, Whose name is the LORD of hosts; And your Redeemer is the Holy One of Israel, Who is called the God of all the earth" (NKJV). Trust God and cling to Him, and His word. Believe that He is there for you, and He will fulfill your every desire. If you do not look to Him, but continue looking out to the world and comparing yourself to others, you are setting yourself up to allow the enemy to step in. That is exactly what happened to me. I looked and I longed. Even though I was in church, I was vulnerable and fell.

IF YOU KNOW BETTER, YOU FALL HARDER

If you are a Christian and are thinking of doing something that you *know* is against the word of God, I cannot say it loud enough, don't do it! A Christian will fall ten times harder than a non-Christian because a Christian *knows* better. You know the word of God, and you hear Him behind you saying go this way, away from the temptation. You will have to purposely turn your back on God to sin. Isaiah 30:21 says, "Whether you turn to the right or to the left, your ears will hear a voice behind you, saying, 'This is the way; walk in it'" (NIV).

We all know that still small voice that tells us not to do something that we know is wrong. That is *not* the little cartoon of the devil on one shoulder and the angel on the other, *it is the Holy Spirit* directing you. When you willfully ignore that voice, you put yourself in a dangerous place. When I ignored God, I put myself and my children in that dangerous place, and we *all* paid the price. Just like Abraham, Sarah, Hagar, Ishmael, and Isaac paid a price enduring enmity and being separated as a family.

I was in "willful sin." Hebrews 10:26-27 says, "For if we go on sinning willfully after receiving the knowledge of the truth, there no longer remains a sacrifice for sins, but a terrifying expectation of judgement and THE FURY OF A FIRE WHICH CONSUME THE ADVERSARIES" (NASB). What a terrible and frightening place I put myself in. I risked my relationship with my children and with God by willfully sinning. None of it was worth it and it has now taken years to rebuild what was torn down.

God has the best in mind for you. You need to know this especially during times of weakness and loneliness. Knowing your worth in Christ will keep you from falling into temptation, but only by seeking Him can we find strength. As the scripture says, our goodness is nothing apart from Him. We can only sustain for so long on our own. We need to seek God for His strength.

Chapter 4
STUDY GUIDE

REFLECT Do you believe it is a weakness or a strength to depend on God to change you?

Have you tried to change areas of your life on your own but could not?

What are those areas and can you trust them to Jesus to help you change?

Have you made promises to God that you were unable to keep?

Are you willing to wait on God and allow Him to build your faith?

READ John 6:63 "It is the Spirit who gives life; the flesh is no help at all. The words that I have spoken to you are spirit and life."

Psalms 16:2 "O my soul, you have said to the Lord, You are my Lord, My goodness is nothing apart from You."

Isaiah 40:30-31 "Even the youths shall faint and be weary, and the young men shall utterly fall: But they that wait upon the LORD shall renew their strength; they shall mount up with wings as eagles; they shall run, and not be weary; and they shall walk, and not faint.

Proverbs 3:5-6 "Trust in the Lord with all your heart, and lean not on your own understanding; In all your ways acknowledge Him, and He shall direct your paths."

DECLARE God understands my weaknesses. The Bible is full of imperfect men and women. Jesus is the only perfect One. He wants to carry me through my times of struggle. I cannot do it on my own. He is my ultimate source of power and strength. I will trust Him and wait on Him. He will never fail me.

PRAY Jesus, I bring to You today my weakness of _____. I have tried so many times to change on my own but have failed. I realize now that I cannot do it without You. I surrender my will to You, Jesus. I put my trust in You. I ask you to strengthen me and to help me conquer _____. I will trust You and wait upon You as you strengthen me in this battle. Help me to understand that it is not a weakness, but a strength to rely upon You. Lift up my heart as I lay these things before you. Thank you for loving me enough to see me change. In Jesus' name I pray. Amen.

Chapter 5
UNDER THE INFLUENCE

*"No temptation has overtaken you except what is common to mankind.
And God is faithful; he will not let you be tempted beyond what you can bear. But
when you are tempted, he will also provide a way out so that you can endure it."*
1 Corinthians 10:13 (NIV)

One morning as I awoke, I heard God asking me to share a memory that I did not want to share, something that I'm deeply ashamed of. I asked God, "can't we just skip over that part?" As I heard Him speak to me, I realized my temporary moment of embarrassment is nothing if it is something that God wants to use to help someone out of their trouble. And according to this scripture, I am seeking Him, and I have no reason to be ashamed; Psalms 34:4-5, "I sought the Lord, and he answered me; he delivered me from all my fears. Those who look to Him are radiant; their faces are never covered with shame" (NIV).

CHOICES
When we are in a relationship that we know is wrong there will be many warnings to tell you "this isn't right." Again, as it says in Isaiah 30:21, "Whether you turn to the right or to the left, your ears will hear a voice behind you saying, 'This is the way; walk in it'" (NIV). In your subconscious or in your spirit, you know right from wrong.

So, what do you do when someone you want to be in a relationship with, or anyone asks you to do something that you know you should not do? Whether you are underage and it is alcohol, or you are any age, and it is drugs? Are you strong enough to say no; or do you want to be in that relationship so badly that you go against what you know to be right? Does the one offering you the alcohol or the drugs care about those things more than they care about you? You hear the voice behind you as the scripture says, "no, go the other way;" but you don't. That is when we are under the influence of the enemy.

That is what I did when my ex-husband offered me drugs for the first time. I allowed the power of his influence to pull me in the wrong direction. Notice I said *"allowed."* I had a choice, no one forced me. I chose to do what I knew to be wrong. I want to stop here and say, there may be some of you who are reading this who *were* forced against your will. I know that victims of human trafficking are forced against their will to take drugs to break their defenses. This is no fault of their own. If this is you right now, God knows that you are innocent, and He will heal and restore you!

SUBSTANCE ABUSE

I had heard of cocaine, mostly on the news, but never in my wildest thoughts did I ever think about doing it. I wasn't even sure of what it was. I'll never forget the feeling of shock when he asked me. I wanted to ask him to leave, but instead I sat there in disbelief. He didn't force it on me, he just began asking me if I had ever done it. I, of course, said "no." He said it was just like coffee, a caffeine high. I asked him to leave that night and did not do it. But after seeing him again and wanting to stay in the relationship, I eventually gave in and tried it. I did it twice with him; once before we had our son, and once after. The second time I did it, I felt horrible, so low. I realized how highly addictive it was; and that I had an addictive personality. It frightened me, because I wanted more. I looked at our son who we had by then and realized how foolish I was being. I could lose my son and my daughter if I got caught doing this. What if I became addicted and had them taken away from me? It must have been God speaking to me and thankfully I never did it again.

We were married by then and I told him to never bring it around us again. I am blessed that I was able to resist the temptation to become deeper involved in drugs. Drugs and addiction, we all know, ruin our lives. I know many people who have not had the strength as I did to walk away. I am not proud of how I allowed my life to be influenced at the time. Through emotional and physical abuse, drugs were just one more way the enemy wanted to destroy our future.

I have family and friends who have lost loved ones to addiction. Lives are cut short, dreams are vanquished, and grief is left behind. When and how will it end? Only when we realize that we are worth more than a drug or a drink and we give our lives totally to Christ. Addiction to any substance will cause you to steal from those you love. It allows you to disregard another person's wellbeing, cover up, lie, and manipulate in order to get a fix. It destroys love, trust, and breaks bonds. I have witnessed these things firsthand. The substance numbs you from whatever pain you are experiencing in the moment only to bring new pain.

SAMSON'S WEAKNESS

In the book of Judges, Samson was not addicted to a substance but fell twice under the influence of a woman. It cost him dearly. I don't know if he was weak emotionally or addicted to pleasing a woman, but he was heavily influenced in both situations. In Judges chapter 14 Samson's weakness to his new wife cost him his wife and her life. During their seven-day marriage feast Samson challenged his male companions with a riddle. If they could not answer the riddle by the end of the seven days, then they would owe Samson the clothes and linens of 30 men. Judges 14: 12-14, "Let me tell you a riddle," Samson said to them. "If you can give me the answer within the seven days of the feast, I will give you thirty linen garments and thirty sets of clothes. If you can't tell me the answer, you must give me thirty linen garments and thirty sets of clothes. 'Tell us your riddle,' they said. 'Let's hear it.' He replied, 'Out of the eater, something to eat; out of the strong, something sweet'" (NIV).

Samson was referring to a lion he had slain in secret. Not realizing his own strength, he tore the lion's jaws when it lunged to attack him. Upon passing by the lion's carcass later he saw that bees had made their nest in the lion's body, and there was honey. Samson ate of the honey and gave some of the honey to his parents. This was against a covenant made with God not to touch the carcass of any dead thing. Therefore, he kept this a secret.

On the fourth day of the feast when the men could not answer the riddle, they threatened Samson's betrothed, and also her father's life; that she should get the answer to the riddle for them from Samson. She then begged and manipulated to get the answer to the riddle and gave it to the Philistines.

CONSEQUENCES OF OUR CHOICES

Judges 14:15-16, "On the fourth a day, they said to Samson's wife, 'Coax your husband into explaining the riddle for us, or we will burn you and your father's household to death. Did you invite us here to steal our property?' Then Samson's wife threw herself on him, sobbing, 'You hate me! You don't really love me. You've given my people a riddle, but you haven't told me the answer.'

'I haven't even explained it to my father or mother,' he replied, 'so why should I explain it to you?' She cried the whole seven days of the feast. So, on the seventh day he finally told her, because she continued to press him. She in turn explained the riddle to her people" (NIV).

Having lost the bet, Samson left the feast of the marriage in anger and slayed 30 men. While Samson was gone his wife was given to one of his companions. Upon his return he found out that his new wife had been given to another man. He burned with rage and set fire to their vineyards, grains, and olive groves. Samson was an Israelite who married a Philistine woman. They were enemies and, in revenge for Samson's burning their harvest, the Philistines burned his wife and her father. There was a horrible loss of life and blessings because Samson gave into the influence of his weakness, his wife.

DELILAH

In Judges chapter 16 the same weakness cost him his strength, his eyesight, his freedom, and his life. Samson met another Philistine woman named Delilah and fell in love with her. Knowing that Samson was an enemy of the Philistines, the rulers went to Delilah and bribed her with silver to get the secret to Samson's strength. Judges 16:4-6, "Sometime later, he fell in love with a woman in the Valley of Sorek whose name was Delilah. The rulers of the Philistines went to her and said, 'See if you can lure him into showing you the secret of his great strength and how we can overpower him so we may tie him up and subdue him. Each one of us will give you eleven hundred shekels of silver.' So, Delilah said to Samson, 'Tell me the secret of your great strength and how you can be tied up and subdued'" (NIV).

Samson lied to her three times about the secret of his strength, each time Delilah tried to capture him and weaken him for the Philistines. You would think that Samson would understand that she doesn't love him but is instead manipulating him to find his weaknesses. But like any of us who are caught in an addiction, we want to believe that the person loves us despite what is right before our eyes. Just like the substance that gives you a temporary high that you don't want to let go of, in the end there is death. Delilah is finally successful in learning the secrets of Samson's strength and he is captured by the Philistines, his eyes are gouged out, and he is thrown into prison.

Judges 16:15-21, "Then she said to him, 'How can you say, 'I love you,' when you won't confide in me? This is the third time you have made a fool of me and haven't told me the secret of your great strength.' With such nagging she prodded him day after day until he was sick to death of it.

So, he told her everything. No razor has ever been used on my head,' he said, 'because I have been a Nazirite dedicated to God from my mother's womb. If my head were shaved, my strength would leave me, and I would become as weak as any other man.' When Delilah saw that he had told her everything, she sent word to the rulers of the Philistines, 'Come back once more; he has told me everything.' So, the rulers of the

Philistines returned with the silver in their hands. After putting him to sleep on her lap, she called for someone to shave off the seven braids of his hair, and so began to subdue him. And his strength left him. Then she called, 'Samson, the Philistines are upon you!' He awoke from his sleep and thought, 'I'll go out as before and shake myself free.' But he did not know that the Lord had left him. Then the Philistines seized him, gouged out his eyes and took him down to Gaza. Binding him with bronze shackles, they set him to grinding grain in the prison" (NIV).

The Book of Judges goes on to explain Samson's last plight with the Philistines when he destroyed their temple and all who were in it. God answers Samson's prayers for one more chance and returns his strength to him one last time. Sadly, Samson dies in the temple as it comes down.

WE CAN'T CONTINUE LIKE THIS

God was still able to fulfill his will through Samson, and God never gave up on him. But had Samson resisted temptation and the influence of ungodly women, it is likely he would have lived out a long and prosperous life. Just like Samson, continuing in our addiction will bind us, blind us, and break us.

What are you addicted to? What is influencing you and holding you back from God's perfect will in your life? Is it drugs, alcohol, sexual addictions, anger, lust, or pornography? You might go in thinking, "A little porn doesn't hurt. I'm just looking, I'm not actually doing anything." But what you are doing is polluting your mind and spirit and God cannot dwell in a place where lust and sin reside. Many of the people in pornographic videos are victims of human trafficking and forced into sexual servitude. When watching pornography, you are witnessing not only a sexual act, but someone losing their soul.

What will you give up for the next high, the next one-night stand? Will you give up your children? Will you risk your job, your freedom, your life? How far will you chase that empty dream? How many times will you allow the enemy to keep you from your true destiny in Christ? The drugs, the alcohol, the anger, the addictions, the abortions will all pull you away from your true calling in Christ.

ADDICTION: A RAVENOUS LION

1 Peter 5:8-9 says Satan is like a roaring lion seeking whom he may devour, "Be alert and of sober mind. Your enemy the devil prowls around like a roaring lion looking for someone to devour. Resist him, standing firm in the faith, because you know that the family of believers throughout the world is undergoing the same kind of sufferings" (NIV). Addiction is like a ravenous lion. It will rob you of life like an unquenchable soul. It rips apart its prey, it eats, and then it needs to hunt again. Feeding your addiction is like feeding a roaring lion who is never satisfied.

Jesus is the Lion of Judah, and the Bible says the lion will lay down with the lamb in complete peace. A lion is one of the most beautiful and majestic animals created by God, yet it is powerful and vicious. Who will you choose today? Will you choose the roaring lion who seeks to devour you and your life? The addiction that you satisfy for a moment then need to get up and feed again? It will never be satisfied until it takes you down to the pit of hell with its claws ripping you and your loved ones apart. Or will you choose the Lion of Judah, who will quiet the roaring lion and bring you peace?

It may seem impossible or too late to stop and change, but Jesus is there waiting to pull you over that wall. He is waiting to get you to the other side where you will find true happiness and freedom in your life. A place where you will find that you did not need those things in the first place. You will see how they stole from you and begin to see God restore all that was lost.

JUST DO IT!

God promises in Isaiah 61:7, "Instead of your shame you will receive a double portion, and instead of disgrace you will rejoice in your inheritance. And so you will inherit a double portion in your land, and everlasting joy will be yours" (NIV). And in Deuteronomy 30:3-14, "God, your God, will restore everything you lost; he'll have compassion on you; he'll come back and pick up the pieces from all the places where you were scattered. No matter how far away you end up, God, your God, will get you out of there and bring you back to the land your ancestors once possessed. It will be yours again. He will give you a good life and make you more numerous than your ancestors. God, your God, will cut away the thick calluses on your heart and your children's hearts, freeing you to love God, your God, with your whole heart and soul and live, really live. God, your God, will put all these curses on your enemies who hated you and were out to get you. And you will make a new start, listening obediently to God, keeping all his commandments that I'm commanding you today. God, your God, will outdo himself in making things go well for you: you will have babies, get calves, grow crops, and enjoy an all-around good life. Yes, God will start enjoying you again, making things go well for you just as he enjoyed doing it for your ancestors. But only if you listen obediently to God, your God, and keep the commandments and regulations written in this Book of Revelation. Nothing half-hearted here; you must return to God, your God, totally, heart and soul, holding nothing back. This commandment that I am commanding you today isn't too much for you, it's not out of your reach. It's not on a high mountain - you do not have to get mountaineers to climb the peak and bring it down to your level and explain it before you can live it. And it's not across the ocean - you do not have to send sailors out to get it, bring it back, and then explain it before you can live it. No. The word is right here and now-as near as the tongue in your mouth, as near as the heart in your chest. Just do it!" (MSG).

What a beautiful scripture. What beautiful promises! You do not have to seek out the blessings of God, they are not on a high mountain, or across the sea. They are as near as the heart in your chest. We thought that a popular shoe company coined the expression "Just do it!" but it looks like God said it first! You only need to turn to Him and accept Him now. "Just do it!"

THE CYCLE OF VIOLENCE

"He delivers me from my enemies.
You also lift me up above those who rise against me;
You have delivered me from the violent man"
Psalms 18:48 (NKJV)

I'll never forget the confusion I felt the first time I saw my ex-husband demonstrate how he felt toward me. He took a new jacket of mine, threw it on the floor, and used it as a floor mat to wipe his muddy work boots. I had never seen anything like that before. This was just one of many ways he would show me that he saw me as worthless. I knew that I was worth more and that Jesus loved me but hearing that I was worthless time and time again began to wear me down. Out of nowhere he would just call me "a worthless ____" with expletives behind it. This especially accelerated after I lost my job due to a car accident. I no longer was worth anything to him, because to him I was only worth my paycheck.

My children and I endured psychological, emotional, and physical abuse. He never actually hit me, but he would shove me and knock me into walls when he walked by. He once chased me down in his car, almost running me off the road. At the end, before I was finally able to leave him for good, I was convinced he would find a way to end my life. Even after I left, I was always on the lookout watching for him. There were many restraining orders that were broken and many threats. The fear of living with him was real, but so was the fear of leaving. He would always say, "you don't want to see what will happen if you divorce me."

TIME ALONE WITH GOD

It was good that I had those eleven years alone with God. It gave me the strength to get through what I did not know was ahead of me, a marriage filled with abuse and a very long divorce. Perhaps God was strengthening Abraham, when he had 13 years alone with God after Ishmael was born and before the promise of Isaac came to pass. I'm sure that during those 13 years Abraham had time to reflect with God on what he had done. It probably gave him and his family the time they needed to heal and to grow. Maybe it gave them time to learn to get along with one another: he, Sarah, Hagar, and Ishmael. But after Isaac was born, he would need to gather his strength to not only see his family split apart once again, but to obey God when he was asked to offer his long-awaited son Isaac as a sacrifice.

Genesis 22: 1-2, "Sometime later God tested Abraham. He said to him, 'Abraham!' 'Here I am,' he replied. Then God said, 'Take your son, your only son, whom you love—Isaac—and go to the region of Moriah. Sacrifice him there as a burnt offering on a mountain I will show you'" (NIV).

Genesis 22:9-12, "When they reached the place God had told him about, Abraham built an altar there and arranged the wood on it. He bound his son Isaac and laid him on the altar, on top of the wood. Then he reached out his hand and took the knife to slay his son. But the angel of the Lord called out to him from heaven, 'Abraham! Abraham!' 'Here I am,' he replied. 'Do not lay a hand on the boy,' he said. 'Do not do anything to him. Now I know that you fear God, because you have not withheld from me your son, your only son.' Abraham looked up and there in a thicket he saw a ram caught by its horns. He went over and took the ram and sacrificed it as a burnt offering instead of his son" (NIV).

I'm sure when God asked Abraham to make this sacrifice he reflected on his past, and all of the times that he *didn't* listen to God. It would take all of his strength to go up that mountain and obey God, not wanting to miss God's call again. Now I was in the fight of my life; in order to leave the marriage, I needed to rely on all of the strength I had inside of me from the eleven years I had alone with God. It was a very long climb up that mountain, but just like God met Abraham there, God met me and gave me supernatural strength.

EVERYONE GOES DOWN

The cycle of violence is hard to escape. The grasp on your mind through fear is powerful. I was afraid that if I divorced him, I would have to leave our then three-year-old son alone with him. That kept me in the cycle for a long time. I would think, "I would rather be there to protect my son than leave him alone with him." Your mind and your thinking become sick in domestic violence situations. I packed up the kids and left many times only to go back; either because I wanted to believe it could get better or because of the fear of what divorce would bring. I had no legal right to take my stepdaughter when I would leave; and many times I would go back to take the abuse because in my mind I was protecting my son who had to be alone with him.

It sounds sick because it was. This is what happens when you allow fear instead of faith to control your emotions and decisions. When my daughter finally became a teenager, she left. It was another time that she had hope that we would have peace. I had him removed from the home by the courts; but I allowed him to convince me to let him come back. My daughter says today that she didn't run away, she escaped. She is right.

The cycle of violence is a slippery slope, and it pulls everyone in the home down with it. You suffer, your children suffer, and if the cycle is not broken generations will suffer. My daughter was only eleven years old when I met my ex-husband. The eleven years I spent waiting on God were the eleven years I spent raising her and my oldest daughter alone. I look now at my eleven-year-old granddaughter and realize just how young and vulnerable my daughter was. I would have done anything to take care of her and protect her then, so I ask myself now how I could have allowed her to go through this. This is something I never thought or imagined could happen. I am thankful that I know I am a new creation in Christ. Suffering can impact generations, but there is healing for generations!

DELIVERED

I lived in the book of Psalms and Proverbs during this time. Psalms speaks of deliverance and Proverbs speaks of what a wise and godly man should look like. They both gave me hope and strength. As David cried out to God during battle, I cried out to God for help. I held onto Psalm Chapter18, especially verses 47-49, "It is God who avenges me, and subdues the peoples under me; He delivers me from my enemies. You also lift me up above those who rise against me; You have delivered me from the violent man. Therefore, I will give thanks to You, O Lord, among the Gentiles, and sing praises to Your name" (NKJV).

When I would read verse 48, *"You have delivered me from the violent man,"* it would give me hope. I had not yet been delivered, but it said in past tense that I *was* delivered. The scripture ends in praise for what has already been done. I knew that someday I would read that verse, and it would be true. It would be my "past tense" as it is today. It is so important to see the strength of God in His word and that He is fighting for you. If you are struggling and afraid or alone right now, know that God is on your side. He hears your cry and is ready to deliver you. God's words are far more important than mine and only He can offer true hope.

Living in an abusive relationship plays many tricks on your mind. In my opinion, this was the ultimate failure: a very bad marriage that I thought I could make better. I fell into the cycle of the fear of leaving, and the false hope that it will get better. The longing for a home and a family kept me trapped. Escaping the cycle of violence is a very deep, psychological game. It is easy to look at someone and say, "why don't they just leave?" But fear is a very real thing, a very real trap. Thankfully, through a lot of prayer, I was able to get away for good; but it took years, and the games did not stop. Unfortunately, my fears would be realized as he used our son, not returning him home from visitation many times. There were many court hearings, savings used up, and years spent trying to fix what should have never been broken. This is the result of not waiting on God. The good news is even though so many mistakes were made, God never left. He was always there.

I am not advocating for divorce, but if you are in an abusive relationship, know that God does not expect you to be a victim of abuse. You need to find a safe place to work it out. We tried counseling, but the violent explosions just continued. I struggled a lot with the teaching that the only reason for a divorce is adultery. Although I did have suspicions that he was cheating, I wasn't sure; so, believing that adultery was the only reason I could divorce kept me confused. After seeking God in prayer and through a lot of confirmation, I was able to go.

THE WAY OF LOVE

God calls a man to love his wife as Christ loves the church, and He calls *all of us* to *walk in the way of love*. Ephesians 5:1 says, "Follow God's example, therefore, as dearly loved children and walk in the way of love, just as Christ loved us and gave himself up for us as a fragrant offering and sacrifice to God" (NIV). Walking in the way of love does *not* include emotional, physical or sexual abuse. God calls husbands to love their wives as Christ loves the church. Christ is the head of the church, and the church is Christ's body.

The Bible refers to the husband as the head of the home and instructs him to love his wife as he loves his own body. Jesus died for the church, and that is us, his body. Just as we care for and feed our own bodies, Christ cares for us, feeds us, loves us, and nourishes us. He loves us and one day He will return for us, His church, His bride. There is no greater love than the love of Christ, and this is how Christ expects us to love and to be loved, just as He loves the church.

God is not only an image of a Father, but also an image of a husband. Ephesians 5:25-30, "Husbands, love your wives, just as Christ loved the church and gave himself up for her to make her holy, cleansing her by the washing with water through the word, and to present her to himself as a radiant church, without stain or wrinkle or any other blemish, but holy and blameless. In this same way, husbands ought to love their wives as their own bodies. He who loves his wife loves himself. After all, no one ever hated their own body, but they feed and care for their body, just as Christ does the church for we are members of his body" (NIV).

Christ gave Himself up for us and died for us, His Church, so that we could live. God is commanding you to love your wife just as He loves the church. Just as He loves you and me. John 15:13 says, "Greater love has no one than this, than to lay down one's life for his friends" (NKJV). Christ is our friend who laid His life down for us so that we might live.

Stop living life being hurt or hurting those around you. Make the change today. Follow the example of Jesus.

WHERE ARE THE MEN?

"So God created mankind in his own image,
in the image of God he created them;
male and female he created them."
Genesis 1:27 (KJV)

Recently, I deleted all of my social media accounts to remain focused on completing this book. When I was on certain platforms, I followed several pro-life groups and I noticed that some of the comments were becoming more and more hostile towards women, blaming them for getting pregnant. I don't know whether the people making these comments were pro-life or pro-choice; but if we are pro-woman then why is there so much focus on blaming the mother? Where are the men? Where is their responsibility in the pregnancy? It takes a woman *and* a man to create a life. I am guilty of not holding the men in my life responsible. I had the wrong attitude. I did not believe that I needed a man or that a man could be good. I made a choice to keep men out of my life, and I can only speak for myself.

I don't know if other women are in good or bad relationships; but what I do know is that attitudes toward women seem to be getting worse. One of the comments that I have seen more than once is, "if you keep your legs together, you won't get pregnant." Shockingly, that comment was made by other women. What about the men who did not keep their pants on? This mentality only furthers the burden on women. The woman is pregnant, she is faced with the decision of keeping the baby and raising it alone, giving up the baby, or having an abortion. This is not the plan of God, nor the position He wants women to be in. Sure, just "keep your legs together" is an option. In other words, don't have sex and stay abstinent. I did it for eleven years. As I said earlier without the power of God, our human strength will eventually run out.

AN EASY OUT

Society has given both men and women an easy way out of the responsibility of pregnancy through abortion. Abortion "gets rid of the problem." The moment you realize you are pregnant you cannot see the baby, but you do see the financial commitment, time, and uncertainty of raising a child. Maybe you are young, you feel panic and are afraid to tell your parents. Abortion seems to be the easy and quick solution, and the "problem" is solved; but what is not seen is the life that is lost and the pain that comes afterwards. The forever wondering about your child. Was it a boy or a girl? Counting the days and years of how old he or she would be. When you are unexpectedly pregnant it seems like it will last forever, but in actuality it only lasts nine months. The choice, however, will last a lifetime. Knowing you gave your child life whether you keep the baby or adopt is far easier to deal with than abortion.

Our sexualized society has given us a free ticket to sex for pleasure without commitment. Abortion makes it seem easy to forget the problem and walk away. It takes away the God given command to be responsible as a man, to be a father, and the father image a man is created to be. Abortion eases the man of all responsibility: pay for the abortion and it is over (if he even does that). It also denies the father of any say in the decision. The father could decide he wants the baby, but it's the mother who ultimately makes the decision to have an abortion or not. I recently saw a video on social media of a young father begging and pleading with the mother not to go into a clinic for an abortion. It was a gut-wrenching sight as he cried out loud to save their baby, but he was helpless to stop her. We are stripping ourselves and each other of the right to feel the joy of holding our child.

When we release the father from his responsibility, he can walk away. If the mother wants to keep her baby and he does not want anything to do with the child, she becomes a single parent of a fatherless household. Fatherless homes are a major problem in our country today causing the breakdown of the nuclear family. Thankfully, I can say from the personal experience of being a single mother, by the grace of God, my children

Without the
power of God,
our human
strength will
eventually
run out.

@joygrantofficial
#frommymesstohismasterpiece

have turned out wonderful. Plenty of mistakes were made and, except for my youngest son, they will never know their father, and likewise, my grandchildren will not know their grandfather.

It was one of the most difficult moments of my life when I was asked by a relative to fill out a family tree, and I could not. I was embarrassed that each one of my children had a different father. There is pain and consequence to our sin. My children are a blessing, but because of my own mistakes the broken family tree will follow them. You might think, well then abortion is better than having fatherless children. No, it is not. I would rather face a blank space on the family tree because of a missing father, than face a blank space for my child's name.

THE IMAGE OF GOD

God calls both men and women to honor and serve Him in body, mind, and spirit. God calls men to be the leaders of their households with love and temperance, and to love as He loves the church. If God created a man in His image as it says in Genesis, then what is that image meant to be? What is the image of God reflected as a man in the flesh?

God is patient and kind, compassionate, angers without sin:

> *Psalms 103:8-13, "The LORD is compassionate and merciful, slow to get angry and filled with unfailing love. He will not constantly accuse us, nor remain angry forever. He does not punish us for all our sins; he does not deal harshly with us, as we deserve. For his unfailing love toward those who fear him is as great as the height of the heavens above the earth. He has removed our sins as far from us as the east is from the west. The LORD is like a father to his children, tender and compassionate to those who fear him" (NLT).*

God is a protector and a shield, a stronghold in the day of trouble:

> *Proverbs 18:10, "The name of the LORD is a strong tower; The righteous run to it and are safe" (NKJV).*

Psalms 91:1-2, "Whoever dwells in the shelter of the Most-High will rest in the shadow of the Almighty. I will say of the Lord, 'He is my refuge and my fortress, my God, in whom I trust'" (NIV).

God is a provider:

Matthew 7:9-11, "Which of you, if your son asks for bread, will give him a stone? Or if he asks for a fish, will give him a snake? If you, then, though you are evil, know how to give good gifts to your children, how much more will your Father in heaven give good gifts to those who ask him!" (NIV).

God is a patient and loving teacher:

Psalms 25:12, "Who is the man who fears the Lord? He will instruct him in the way that he should choose" (ESV).

Psalms 32:8, "I will instruct you and teach you in the way which you should go; I will counsel you with My eye upon you" (ESV).

Isaiah 28:6, "For his God instructs and teaches him properly" (NASB).

Isaiah 54:13, "All your children will be taught by the LORD, and great will be their peace" (NIV).

God is a fair and just disciplinarian:

Hebrews 12:5, "My son, do not make light of the Lord's discipline, and do not lose heart when he rebukes you, because the Lord disciplines the one he loves, and he chastens everyone he accepts as his son" (NIV).

Deuteronomy 8:5, "Know then in your heart that as a man disciplines his son, so the LORD your God disciplines you" (NIV).

Job 5:17, "Behold, happy is the person whom God disciplines, so do not reject the discipline of the Almighty" (NASB).

1 Corinthians 11:32, "Yet when we are judged by the Lord, we are being disciplined so that we will not be condemned along with the world" (NLT).

God lovingly leads us and guides us:

Isaiah 48:17, "Thus says the Lord, your Redeemer, the Holy One of Israel, 'I am the Lord your God, who teaches you to profit, Who leads you in the way you should go'" (NKJV).

Deuteronomy 32:9-12, "For the people of Israel belong to the LORD; Jacob is his special possession. He found them in a desert land, in an empty, howling wasteland. He surrounded them and watched over them; he guarded them as he would guard his own eyes. Like an eagle that rouses her chicks and hovers over her young, so he spread his wings to take them up and carried them safely on his pinions. The LORD alone guided them; they followed no foreign gods" (NLT).

God wants the best for us and is patient with us:

2 Peter 3:9, "The Lord is not slow in keeping his promise, as some understand slowness. Instead, he is patient with you, not wanting anyone to perish, but everyone to come to repentance" (NIV).

These are just some of the attributes and characteristics of God. Fathers are not called to be perfect, but an example of God and a reflection of Him. Our homes need mothers *and* fathers. Fathers who strive to be like Christ in the home can lead their families in love and in strength. They and their children will be as the Bible says in Jeremiah, trees planted by living water who are strong and lack for nothing. Jeremiah 17:7-8, "But blessed is the one who trusts in the Lord, whose confidence is in Him. They will be like a tree planted by the water that sends out its roots by the stream. It does not fear when heat comes; its leaves are always green. It has no worries in a year of drought and never fails to bear fruit" (NIV).

CHOOSING JESUS

Men, don't run from the responsibility of your children through abortion or abandonment. Your children need you. God needs you to become the leader of your home that He created you to be. Search the scriptures on your own. Find out who you are called to be in Christ and lead your family to strength and victory. Become strong in the Lord and proud of who you are in Christ. You can treat women as God calls you to treat them, with respect as the Bride of Christ, His church. I don't just think, I know that abstinence *with* the power of God is completely possible. We have to be both men and women committed to God and His power. We must be more in love with Jesus than we are with the idea of sex and flesh. Abstinence sounds old fashioned and impossible. That is just another lie from the enemy. It is empowering and freeing to care for your body as Christ cares for you. It is the power in Christ of not *needing* or *allowing* the desires of our flesh to rule our minds and our bodies.

I have never been more in love with Jesus or more fulfilled in life than I have been the past fifteen years. So, in love that I don't want to disappoint Him. I want to serve Him. The more I serve Him, the more I want to do His will. The more I do His will, the more joy I receive. It is unending and no matter my circumstance, my cup overflows. He is my savior, and He brings me joy and peace that passes all understanding. Why would I let that be taken away from me for a temporary moment of gratification? I wouldn't. I couldn't. I do not want to. I want nothing more than to do His will. I know He *will* give me the desires of my heart.

Galatians 5:16-22 says, "So I say, walk by the Spirit, and you will not gratify the desires of the flesh. For the flesh desires what is contrary to the Spirit, and the Spirit what is contrary to the flesh. They are in conflict with each other, so that you are not to do whatever you want. But if you are led by the Spirit, you are not under the law. The acts of the flesh are obvious: sexual immorality, impurity and debauchery; idolatry and witchcraft; hatred, discord, jealousy, fits of rage, selfish ambition, dissensions, factions and envy; drunkenness, orgies, and the like. I warn you, as I did before, that those who live like this will not inherit the kingdom of God. But the fruit of the Spirit is love, joy, peace, forbearance, kindness, goodness, faithfulness, gentleness and self-control. Against such things there is no law. Those who belong to Christ Jesus have crucified the flesh with its passions and desires. Since we live by the Spirit, let us keep in step with the Spirit. Let us not become conceited, provoking and envying each other" (NIV).

Live by the spirit of God and find His love, peace, joy, strength, and freedom.

Chapter 5
STUDY GUIDE

REFLECT Is there something in your life that you know is wrong, but you are justifying it to keep doing it?

Can you hand that thing to Jesus and allow Him to remove it from your life, no matter the risk?

Are you clinging to an unhealthy relationship or influence?

If yes, will you allow Jesus to show you how to get healthy and/or find safety if it is necessary?

Can you strive to be more like God and reflect His positive attributes?

READ 1 Corinthians 10:13 "No temptation has overtaken you except what is common to mankind. And God is faithful; he will not let you be tempted beyond what you can bear. But when you are tempted, he will also provide a way out so that you can endure it."

Psalms 18:48 "He delivers me from my enemies. You also lift me up above those who rise against me; You have delivered me from the violent man."

Psalms 34:4-5 "I sought the Lord, and he answered me; he delivered me from all my fears. Those who look to Him are radiant; their faces are never covered with shame."

Isaiah 30:21 "Whether you turn to the right or to the left, your ears will hear a voice behind you saying, 'This is the way; walk in it.'"

2 Corinthians 12:9 "My grace is sufficient for you, for my power is made perfect in weakness."

Ephesians 5:1 "Follow God's example, therefore, as dearly loved children and walk in the way of love, just as Christ loved us and gave himself up for us as a fragrant offering and sacrifice to God."

DECLARE I am more than the struggle that I face in my life. My life is worth living; I have strength and value. There is no temptation that comes against me that I cannot handle when I call on the Name of Jesus. He will guide me and walk me through it, to conquer it and make me whole. My hands were not created for evil, but for good. Therefore, I will seek God to use me for good and to be more like Him.

PRAY Father, I come before You and ask Your forgiveness for _____. Cleanse my heart and my hands. Make me more like you every day. I commit my life to You. I ask You to fill me with Your Holy Spirit that gives me the power and supernatural strength to conquer these things in my life. I thank You for it now, in Jesus' name I pray. Amen.

Chapter 6
LOVE IS NOT SEX, SEX IS NOT LOVE

"For this is the will of God, your sanctification:
that you abstain from sexual immorality"
1 Thessalonians 4:3 (ESV)

How many of us mistake the intimate feeling of sex for love? Sex is not *love*, but rather an *expression of love* meant for marriage. It is the most beautiful and meaningful expression of love that God created for a man and a woman. God gave Adam to Eve, and Eve to Adam. They were the first husband and wife created in a beautiful garden, they had everything they needed. Most of us know their story, they were tempted and fell; but they still had each other. They were married by God Himself. Genesis 4:1 says, "And Adam knew Eve his wife..." (KJV). When the Bible refers to "know" or "knew" in this way, it is referring to the act of sex.

How well do we really know the person we are in a sexual relationship with? The act of sex is an expression of love, but it falls as a very weak foundation if all that you have is a physical relationship. To know someone is to know their strengths, their weaknesses, their likes and dislikes, their talents, their ups and downs, and to love them through them all. When we begin to understand the way God knows and loves us, we will also begin to understand that we are worth more than just a physical relationship. You are worth being loved.

Think of some of the ways God "knows" us:

> *He knows us by name. Exodus 33:17, "And the LORD said to Moses, 'I will do the very thing you have asked, because I am pleased with you and I know you by name'" (NIV). The God who created the Heavens and the earth, who is omnipotent and present from the beginning to the end of time knows us by name. That is intimate.*

> *He knows our needs. Matthew 6:8, "…. your Father knows what you need before you ask him" (NIV).*

> *He knows us intimately and loves us. 1 Corinthians 8:3, "But if anyone loves God, he is known by God" (ESV).*

> *He knows us as His own. John 10:14, "I am the good shepherd, and I know My own and My own know Me" (NASB). He recognizes us and acknowledges us.*

> *He knows us and leads us. John 10:27, "My sheep hear My voice, and I know them, and they follow Me" (NKJV). He wants the best for us.*

> *He knows us and protects us. Nahum 1:7, "The LORD is good, A stronghold in the day of trouble, And He knows those who take refuge in Him" (NASB).*

> *He knows us and gives us access to His Father. Matthew 11:27, "All things have been handed over to me by my Father, and no one knows the Son except the Father, and no one knows the Father except the Son and anyone to whom the Son chooses to reveal him" (ESV).*

> *He lays His life down for those that He knows. John 10:15, "As the Father knows Me, even so I know the Father; and I lay down My life for the sheep" (NKJV). There is no greater love or sacrifice than one who lays His life down for another.*

These are just some of the ways Christ knows us and each one is intimate. Now think about the person that you are with or have been with, how well do you know them? How well do they know you, and how well do you really know yourself? Are we giving ourselves away outside of marriage to people we don't really know? Are we taking the time to get to know God, or even ourselves?

LIVING TOGETHER

When I met my ex-husband, I didn't know my worth in Christ, and I did not take the time to get to know him. Instead, once again I gave myself away for what I thought I was worth. I had a fundamental flaw in believing that sex before marriage was okay and even normal. I knew that the Bible said sex was for marriage and it was preached in church; even though that felt right to me, it did not seem possible. It may even feel that way to you as you read this. It was accepted around me, even in the church, and it did not seem reasonable to wait until marriage. I thought it would be nice and I wanted to wait, but it was more like a fairy tale than a reality.

After all, I had waited eleven years, and nothing was happening. As I became involved with him, things began to go from bad to worse. I became pregnant with our son and out of desperation we began living together. Now in my thirties, I could not bear to be a single mom again. Living together was something that I said I would never do, but I found myself doing it.

Paul says in Romans 7:15-20, "I do not understand what I do. For what I want to do I do not do, but what I hate I do. And if I do what I do not want to do, I agree that the law is good. As it is, it is no longer I myself who do it, but it is sin living in me. For I know that good itself does not dwell in me, that is, in my sinful nature. For I have the desire to do what is good, but I cannot carry it out. For I do not do the good I want to do, but the evil I do not want to do—this I keep on doing. Now if I do what I do not want to do, it is no longer I who do it, but it is sin living in me that does it" (NIV). In other words, if we allow it, our sinful nature is going to take over and cause us to do the things we do not want to do. The very last thing I wanted to do was to live with a man, but now I had put myself into a position that I felt I had no way out of. I had my daughter at home with me, I was pregnant, and I was going to lose my job. I needed help, but the help I looked for was not the help that I needed. I needed help from the Lord.

God says we are to be married and I constantly felt the weight of that conviction on my life. I was embarrassed that I had put my daughter in the position of living in a bad situation. I allowed guilt and shame to push me into getting married and once again dreams were stolen. There was no wedding, but instead, a quick marriage at the courthouse that ended in disaster. Taking matters into my own hands, I wanted to "make things right" in the eyes of God and my children, but it did not make anything better. I was not with the person that God had planned for me and even if I was, it was not done according to His will.

WHO ARE WE IMITATING?

I am speaking to Christians now. I wonder how many of you are living together, sleeping together and going to church as though you are married. You hide it but inside you know that you are not living right. I would venture to say it is almost the norm and it should not be. We are called to be different and examples of the light of Christ. Ephesians 5:1-3 says we are to be imitators of Christ without sexual immorality among us, "Therefore be imitators of God, as beloved children. And walk in love, as Christ loved us and gave himself up for us, a fragrant offering and sacrifice to God. But sexual immorality and all impurity or covetousness must not even be named among you, as is proper among saints" (ESV).

Are we imitating Christ or are we imitating the world? If we imitate the world, we are no longer witnesses for Christ, but we are like the world. As a matter of fact, the Bible says in 1 Corinthians 6:13-20 that we are actually joining our body, which is part of Christ's body as a Christian, to sexual sin: "You say, 'Food was made for the stomach, and the stomach for food.' (This is true, though someday God will do away with both of them.) But you cannot say that our bodies were made for sexual immorality. They were made for the Lord, and the Lord cares about our bodies. And God will raise us from the dead by his power, just as he raised our Lord from the dead. Don't you realize that your bodies are actually parts of Christ? Should a man take his body, which is part of Christ, and join it to a prostitute (sexual immorality)? Never! And don't you realize that if a man joins himself to a prostitute, he becomes one body with her? For the Scriptures say, 'The two are united into one.' But the person who is joined to the Lord is one spirit with him. Run from sexual sin! No other sin so clearly affects the body as this one does. For sexual immorality is a sin against your own body. Don't you realize that your body is the temple of the Holy Spirit, who lives in you and was given to you by God? You do not belong to yourself, for God bought you with a high price. So you must honor God with your body" (NLT).

WE ARE CREATIONS OF THE MOST-HIGH GOD

If you are living together, you are probably thinking, "What are we supposed to do, move out and change everything? It's expensive, we can't!" It might even be a ridiculous thought in a society where it is the norm to live together before marriage. We make ourselves into objects like a car and "test each other out" to see if we will work going for a test drive. We are not objects; we are creations of the Most-High God. We are the sons and the daughters of Jesus Christ. Ephesians 2:10 says, "For we are his workmanship, created in Christ Jesus for good works, which God prepared beforehand, that we should walk in them" (ESV). When we are not walking in the fullness of Christ, we cannot fully recognize the good works He has prepared for us to do. He cannot use us as a witness to the world when we ourselves are behaving like the world. We are called to be different.

If you love the person you are with, then you will hold them in the highest place of honor in marriage. You will commit your life to them for better or for worse, no matter what it takes. Move out for a season, date again, and abstain from sex. Sex is not a requirement in dating. Today after the third date, there is pressure to "put out" as if you owe someone something for a few nights out to dinner. We sell ourselves short of what God has intended for us.

It will not be easy, but it is not impossible. Instead of running to each other when things get passionate, run to Jesus. Get on your knees and ask for strength. If you find it is impossible and you are deeply in love, then do as the scripture says, and get married. I recommend the first, move out, date, and fall in love again. Get to know each other for who you really are. But as Paul says in 1 Corinthians 7:8-9, if it seems impossible to you then marry, "Now to the unmarried and the widows I say: It is good for them to stay unmarried, as I do. But if they cannot control themselves, they should marry, for it is better to marry than to burn with passion" (NIV).

THE BIBLE

Jesus came to change the world. All throughout Roman history there was ruthlessness, murder, and the oppression of God's people. Jesus came with a new idea. He brought heaven to earth. What we now know as our Western society is based on the teachings of Jesus Christ. He brought freedom, prosperity, and democracy. He did not die so that we could do what we want to do. He took on the sins of the world. Imagine the darkness He felt on the cross. Everything that you or I have done or will do was on His shoulders. He bore the sins of every person who exists, has existed, and has yet to exist. He bore the chastisement of our sins. It was the only time the Father turned His face away from His Son.

In His death and resurrection, He brought hope and forgiveness for those sins. He gave each one of us a new chance at freedom and a clean heart. A clean slate, a new beginning. The Bible is full of hope, forgiveness, and guidelines for living. When we ignore those guidelines and think that we can just do as we decide, we say, "thank you Jesus for the forgiveness of my sin, but I'd like to just keep this sin over here, or that sin over there." It's time once again to allow Jesus to change us and our society. A society that has made its way into His church, His Bride.

Jesus gave each
one of us a new
chance at freedom
and a clean heart.

A clean slate.

A new beginning.

@joygrantofficial
#frommymesstohismasterpiece

A SPOTLESS BRIDE

*"Husbands, love your wives, just as Christ
loved the church and gave himself up for her"*
Ephesians 5:25 (NIV)

Jesus is returning for His church, a spotless Bride. Jesus refers to himself as the husband coming for His bride and once again marriage is honored. It is time to take a stand, be strong, and honor what Jesus did for us on the cross. In John 4:4-26, when Jesus met the woman at the well, she had multiple husbands and was living with a man. Jesus revealed himself to her as the Messiah and He gave her new life:

"Now he had to go through Samaria. So, he came to a town in Samaria called Sychar, near the plot of ground Jacob had given to his son Joseph. Jacob's well was there, and Jesus, tired as he was from the journey, sat down by the well. It was about noon. When a Samaritan woman came to draw water, Jesus said to her, 'Will you give me a drink?' (His disciples had gone into the town to buy food.) The Samaritan woman said to him, 'You are a Jew and I am a Samaritan woman. How can you ask me for a drink?' (For Jews do not associate with Samaritans.) Jesus answered her, 'If you knew the gift of God and who it is that asks you for a drink, you would have asked him and he would have given you living water.'

'Sir,' the woman said, 'you have nothing to draw with and the well is deep. Where can you get this living water? Are you greater than our father, Jacob, who gave us the well and drank from it himself, as did also his sons and his livestock?' Jesus answered, 'Everyone who drinks this water will be thirsty again, but whoever drinks the water I give them will never thirst. Indeed, the water I give them will become in them a spring of water welling up to eternal life.'

The woman said to him, 'Sir, give me this water so that I won't get thirsty and have to keep coming here to draw water.' He told her, 'Go, call your husband and come back.'

'I have no husband,' she replied. Jesus said to her, 'You are right when you say you have no husband. The fact is, you have had five husbands, and the man you now have is not your husband. What you have just said is quite true.'

'Sir,' the woman said, 'I can see that you are a prophet. Our ancestors worshiped on this mountain, but you Jews claim that the place where we must worship is in Jerusalem.'

'Woman,' Jesus replied, 'believe me, a time is coming when you will worship the Father neither on this mountain nor in Jerusalem. You Samaritans worship what you do not know; we worship what we do know, for salvation is from the Jews. Yet a time is coming and has now come when the true worshipers will worship the Father in the Spirit and in truth, for they are the kind of worshipers the Father seeks. God is spirit, and his worshipers must worship in the Spirit and in truth.'

The woman said, 'I know that Messiah' (called Christ) 'is coming. When he comes, he will explain everything to us.' Then Jesus declared, 'I, the one speaking to you—I am he'" (NIV).

I am sure that after this experience with Jesus at the well, she went home and told her live-in boyfriend that what they were doing was wrong and he needed to move out. She was instantly a new creation in Christ. She had an encounter with the Messiah. John 4:28-29, "Then leaving her water jar, the woman went back to the town and said to the people, 'Come, see a man who told me everything I ever did. Could this be the Messiah?'" (NIV).

Even though Jesus had not yet died for her sins, He was there for her, and she was transformed by His word. He literally spoke new life into her, face to face. There was a need in her for companionship, but for some reason she didn't have that permanent love in a relationship. Jesus met that need for her immediately, just as He met that need for me. He will meet your needs, too.

CULTURE'S VIEW OF SEX
Sex is a normal and beautiful thing, a gift from God for marriage. God gave us the ability to procreate through sex and in doing so He made it

one of the greatest gifts of all. He gave us pleasure and love. He made two flesh become one. In Genesis 2:24 it says, "That is why a man leaves his father and mother and is united to his wife, and they become one flesh. Adam and his wife were both naked, and they felt no shame" (NIV). When we do things God's way there is no shame. I was living a shame-based life. Every relationship decision I made was based on the shame of the past or the shame I was creating in my present. Sex outside of marriage is good for the moment; but when it is over, we are left with shame or hoping for more.

The world has turned sex into an act without love, passion, or commitment. It has turned something beautiful into something that leaves us empty and many times alone. Rather than an expression of love it is turned into lust merely to satisfy a physical need. Sometimes that need is never fulfilled, leading to sexual addictions, pornography, and the abuse of those caught in sexual exploitation. None of these things lead you to God, but away from God.

SEX IS A COMMITMENT

As it says in Galatians 5:19-21, "Now the works of the flesh are evident: sexual immorality, impurity, sensuality, idolatry, sorcery, enmity, strife, jealousy, fits of anger, rivalries, dissensions, divisions, envy, drunkenness, orgies, and things like these. I warn you, as I warned you before, that those who do such things will not inherit the kingdom of God" (ESV) and 1 John 2:15-17, "Do not love the world or anything in the world. If anyone loves the world, love for the Father is not in them. For everything in the world—the lust of the flesh, the lust of the eyes, and the pride of life—comes not from the Father but from the world. The world and its desires pass away, but whoever does the will of God lives forever" (NIV).

Don't allow the tricks of the enemy to pull you away from God the Father and His perfect will for your life. Seek Him in purity and in truth and He will give you the strength you need to abstain. Once you have begun to search God for His strength and His will, the desires of this world pass away and the desire to please Him increases. I know this, because this is how I now live my life. My desire to please God far outweighs my desires for physical love. My faith has increased to know that He will supply my every need, and He will bring that love to my life that I desire. I don't need to go to the world to look for it, I only need to look to Him and His perfect will.

Sex is a binding commitment in marriage created by God. Outside of marriage we have heartache, grief, STDs, unplanned pregnancy, and abortion. God does things for our good and for our protection. When you are married and faithful, there is no chance of contracting an STD from your mate. When you become pregnant, it is your child together, created out of your love. I am not saying that marriages don't have their heartaches, mine did. But there was still a beauty in knowing that I was married when I had sex with my husband at the time. It was something I had never experienced even though the marriage ended in divorce. For a moment I experienced something good as God had intended it. But because it was an abusive marriage, I was missing the true love.

SEXUAL SINS AND THE CHURCH

It is time to stop living together, sleeping together, and *acting* like we are married. I did it. I went to church when my ex and I were living together. I liked the companionship, but knowing I was out of God's will only brought more shame. Let's make a true decision to follow Him and be the examples we are called to be. If it takes moving out, then move out. If you are dating and in a sexual relationship, stop. I ruined my chances of a wedding, of doing life right, and it was my own doing. Like Ishmael, I made my own bad decisions. It has been a long and hard road to recovery from an abusive marriage for both myself and for my children. Why do it? Why put yourself through it when Jesus has a better plan for you? Find that plan, seek Him, and follow it.

Ephesians 5:25-27 says, "Husbands, love your wives, just as Christ loved the church and gave himself up for her to make her holy, cleansing her by the washing with water through the word, and to present her to himself *as a radiant church*, without stain or wrinkle or any other blemish, but holy and blameless" (NIV). Are we "staining" the church with our sexual sins? I'm sounding harsh right now, but I am still talking to my brothers and sisters in Christ who are living life one way inside of the church and another way outside of the church. We are representatives of Christ. We can fool people, but we cannot fool God. He sees us. He knows what we are doing, and He wants the best for us. We cannot represent Christ and sin at the same time. Galatians 2:17 says, "But if, while we seek to be justified by Christ, we ourselves also are found sinners, is Christ therefore a minister of sin? Certainly not!" (NKJV).

When you submit your life to Christ, you are no longer ruled by your desires, but by God's Spirit, who lives in you. Romans 8:7-9, "Our desires fight against God, because they do not and cannot obey God's laws. If we follow our desires, we cannot please God. You are no longer ruled by your desires, but by God's Spirit, who lives in you" (CEV).

LONGING FOR CHRIST
When we give our lives to Christ, we lay down or crucify our "fleshly" desires and He fills us with spiritual desires. Galatians 2:20 says, "I have been crucified with Christ. It is no longer I who live, but Christ who lives in me. And the life I now live in the flesh I live by faith in the Son of God, who loved me and gave himself for me" (ESV). Reaching and searching for something to fill your needs whether it be sex, the hunger for love, drugs, alcohol, money, food, or anything that fills the fleshly needs will leave you empty. It will be a temporary high, a temporary fulfillment in the moment, but the emptiness and shame will still be there waiting when you come down.

I have not been in a relationship since my divorce 15 years ago. This is not because I do not want one, it is because seeking God and His will for my life has become far more important to me. Does that mean the desire is not there? No, it doesn't. It just means that my longing for Christ has become far greater than the longing for my personal needs. I am no longer ruled or driven by my fleshly desires to be loved. Galatians 5:16 says, "So I say, walk by the Spirit, and you will not gratify the desires of the flesh" (NIV). And Romans 8:9, "You are no longer ruled by your desires, but by God's Spirit, who lives in you" (CEV).

I now know and understand that He *will* provide my *every* need: not some of my needs, but *all* of my needs. In committing my life fully to Him, I have peace that I have never known that passes *all* understanding. Philippians 4:6-7, "Do not worry about anything; instead, pray about everything. Tell God what you need and thank him for all he has done. Then you will experience God's peace, which exceeds anything we can understand. His peace will guard your hearts and minds as you live in Christ Jesus" (NLT).

Isaiah 26:3 says, "You will keep in perfect peace all who trust in you, all whose thoughts are fixed on you!" (NLT). When you have a new foundation in Christ it will not fail or fall. This foundation will hold you, support you, and bless you more than you can ever imagine or think because the foundation is in Jesus Christ. It is a foundation that will not crumble, it will not let you down. This is what I want for you. To desire Him above all things in your life and stand on the firm foundation of Christ. He will meet your every desire beyond your imagination. You are worth waiting for! If a man is willing to wait for you and give his desires to God, what love is that! How can I speak to something I have not experienced myself? I can because I know the full love of Christ and His willingness to die for me. He offers me the knowledge of His love and shows me the love that is worth waiting for. If I never experience it in the flesh on earth, I have experienced it now in the spirit and I know I am worth waiting for.

REFLECT Do you believe that a relationship with Jesus can be intimate?

Do you believe or understand that God sets up boundaries not to hinder us, but to protect us?

Do you view abstaining from sex before marriage as an old-fashioned idea or protection from God?

Can you honor the person you are involved with by committing to love them as Christ loves them?

How does Christ love them and how can you emulate Christ's love?

READ 1 Thessalonians 4:3 "For this is the will of God, your sanctification: that you abstain from sexual immorality."

Ephesians 5:1-3 "Therefore be imitators of God, as beloved children. And walk in love, as Christ loved us and gave himself up for us, a fragrant offering and sacrifice to God. But sexual immorality and all impurity or covetousness must not even be named among you, as is proper among saints."

Corinthians 6:13-20 "You say, 'Food was made for the stomach, and the stomach for food.' (This is true, though someday God will do away with both of them.) But you cannot say that our bodies were made for sexual immorality. They were made for the Lord, and the Lord cares about our bodies. And God will raise us from the dead by his power, just as he raised our Lord from the dead. Don't you realize that your bodies are actually parts of Christ? Should a man take his body, which is part of

Christ, and join it to a prostitute (sexual immorality)? Never! And don't you realize that if a man joins himself to a prostitute, he becomes one body with her? For the Scriptures say, 'The two are united into one.' But the person who is joined to the Lord is one spirit with him. Run from sexual sin! No other sin so clearly affects the body as this one does. For sexual immorality is a sin against your own body. Don't you realize that your body is the temple of the Holy Spirit, who lives in you and was given to you by God? You do not belong to yourself, for God bought you with a high price. So you must honor God with your body."

1 Corinthians 7:8-9 "Now to the unmarried and the widows I say: It is good for them to stay unmarried, as I do. But if they cannot control themselves, they should marry, for it is better to marry than to burn with passion."

Philippians 4:13 "I can do all things through Christ who strengthens me."

DECLARE I am more than a sexual relationship and worth waiting for. I do not have to give myself away in order to be loved or to prove my love. True love will wait for me and honor me, just as Jesus waits for and honors me. If I am weak in this area, with Jesus I can do all things. I am created by God to do His good work and to love others just as He loves them.

PRAY Jesus, I commit my soul and my body to you. Help me realize that you created the beauty of marriage, and in marriage there is joy and commitment. As I join myself to the person that I love, we are one in spirit and are one with you. Father, forgive me for any sexual sins that I may have committed. I ask you to fulfill this part of my life and to show me what love should look like. Use my hands and my body for your good works as you created them. I thank you for these things, in Jesus' name I pray. Amen.

Chapter 7
LEARNING TO FORGIVE

"Love those that hate you, forgive those that hurt you."
Reverend Billy Graham

Billy Graham was a modern-day Moses who brought millions of people to Christ. He preached the Gospel of Jesus Christ both unashamed and unafraid. I wish I had heard his teachings growing up, but more than that I wish my father would have listened to him. How different our lives could have been had my father followed the Lord. Recently, I listened to one of Billy Graham's sermons. It was a sermon on forgiveness that was recorded in 1968. I would have been nine years old at the time it was broadcast. It amazes me that what he was saying so long ago still applies as truth today. "Love those that hate you, forgive those that hurt you."

You cannot heal without forgiving. Carrying unforgiveness in your heart only continues to hurt you. Unforgiveness turns into bitterness and feeds negativity which leads to more bad decisions in your life. It will spread like a disease to your relationships and to those around you. Hebrews 12:15 says, "See to it that no one falls short of the grace of God and that no bitter root grows up to cause trouble and defile many" (NIV). Unforgiveness will cause you to "fall short" of the grace of God, in other words, you will miss out on His best for you. It will flow from you to your children and to your relationships. My father was very hurt by life, and very bitter. Many nights, he told us stories of how he was hurt by his mother and left in the orphanage. His hurt was flowing from him to us.

Forgiving is hard. Sometimes it takes a lot of work, but it is something we must do. Mark 11:26 says, "But if you do not forgive, neither will your Father in heaven forgive your trespasses" (NKJV). I understand the things that may be going on in your mind right now. I know because I had to forgive; and it *is* hard, but it is also freeing. We are deceived into thinking that when we forgive someone who hurt us, we are giving them a gift. The truth is when we withhold forgiveness we are destroying ourselves with hurt and anger. It affects our lives, our health, and our relationships. We *think our unforgiveness is punishing* the person who hurt us, when in reality we are punishing ourselves. Not only are we hurting ourselves with anger and bitterness, but we also hurt our relationship with Christ. It makes us say and do ugly things. It takes away from the good character that Christ wants to build in us. It hurts *us*.

I had so much hurt and anger after my divorce that it was too much to bear. I tried to keep it to myself, but the pain was excruciating and almost unexplainable when I would think of things that my ex-husband did to us. I begged God to "take away the pain" but when He told me I would need to forgive in order to heal, I just didn't know how. I knew I had to, I knew God was calling me to, but how? How do you forgive someone who has caused so much pain and grief in your life?

UNFORGIVENESS KEEPS THEM IN YOUR LIFE

I sought God for His help. I wanted to forgive and be free from the pain and the hurt. It felt as though the pain was keeping me bound to my ex-husband; and, if fact, it was. Hurt, unforgiveness, and hatred keep you bound to the very person who you want to be free from. The hurt causes you to think about them and talk about them; it affects your emotions and takes away your time and your energy. You are not really free, you are bound. I wanted freedom. I wanted it all gone. All of it, for mine, and my children's sake.

I was blown away when I heard God's instructions on how to forgive and release this pain. He asked me to do something that seemed

You
can not
heal
without
forgiving.

unfair. God told me to call my ex-husband and tell him that I forgive him and to ask him to forgive me. God told me to tell him that I release what he did to us to God. "Call him and tell him that I forgive him?" I thought, "and to forgive me? Shouldn't he be calling *me* to *ask* for *my* forgiveness?" I quickly realized what I was doing and stopped myself from questioning God and humbled myself instead. This was not the same as writing a letter to someone as I did with the date in California; I wrote that letter to relieve my feelings of guilt and shame. This was God leading me to my own personal healing. I prayed for strength to do it and I also asked why. It is okay to ask God questions, He loves us enough to answer. God told me that I had a part to play in the marriage, too. I knew better as a Christian when I married him. I needed to take responsibility for my part.

FREEDOM

Of course, I knew God was right. I prayed for strength, the right words, and for the right time to call. A few days later I was sitting in my car watching my son practice football, and God spoke to me: "Call him now." My heart began to race, I didn't want to call him. I kept as little communication with him as possible because most conversations ended badly. But in that moment, I prayed for strength and said, "God, I trust you." As I was praying and getting the strength to call, I noticed a man at the end of the football field walking back and forth, pacing the entire width of the football field. I thought, "What is that man doing?" And then I made the call. I said, "God told me that I needed to call you and tell you that I forgive you for everything that you have done to us. That I release you from my unforgiveness and I'm sorry for my part in the relationship." I don't remember all of the conversation; I just know that he was shocked, and it was a short call. When I hung up, I cried, and felt such joy and release. The anger could no longer hurt me, I was free. When football practice was over my son came running up to the car excited that our Pastor's son was on his team. I saw our Pastor walk by and realized that he was the man that I saw pacing the football field. I believe that he was praying right at the time that I made that phone call.

I understand that there are situations where you cannot call the person and talk to them like God instructed me to do. There was a time when I had restraining orders in place against my ex-husband and it simply would not have been safe to call him; but God knew the timing for me. Every situation is going to be different. You have to work out your situation between yourself and God, but you must find a way to forgive. When you walk in unforgiveness you not only hold the person hostage, you are hostage also. You keep it alive inside of you, you think on it, dwell on it, talk about it, it keeps you awake at night. Forgiveness allows the offense to die, and it cannot hurt you anymore.

FORGIVING OTHERS

Colossians 3:13 says, "Bear with each other and forgive one another if any of you has a grievance against someone. Forgive as the Lord forgave you" (NIV). You may not want to let go of the hurt because, depending on the situation, letting go of the pain is like letting go of the person who hurt you. Maybe you are hurt by a spouse who left you for someone else. In some way you still feel connected to him or her by holding on to those emotions. It may feel good for a while, but those emotions will eventually turn into bitterness and block God's ability to heal you. Bitterness and unforgiveness stand in God's way. Just imagine God running to bring you your blessings, and there in front of Him stands a giant wall marked "Bitterness and Unforgiveness," and you are on the other side of that wall. God wants that wall gone so that He can reach you and bless you.

Matthew 5:23-24 says, "Therefore, if you are offering your gift at the altar and there remember that your brother or sister has something against you, leave your gift there in front of the altar. First go and be reconciled to them; then come and offer your gift" (NIV). In other words, get unforgiveness out of your heart before you come to the throne of God, the throne of Grace. Stop and take a moment to ask God to forgive you for carrying unforgiveness and pain that does not belong to you. Ask Him to help you forgive the one or ones who have hurt you and begin to receive God's healing. That is the grace, healing, and freedom He wants to extend to you. John 8:36 says, "So if the Son sets you free, you will be free indeed" (NIV). Forgiving others allows Jesus to set you free!

JESUS FORGAVE

"For if you forgive other people when they sin against you,
your heavenly Father will also forgive you."
Matthew 6:14 (NIV)

Jesus was betrayed by Judas with a kiss. Those whom Jesus loved and ate with, spent time teaching, and laughing with were not to be found on the night of His betrayal. Peter denied Jesus three times before sunrise. Jesus was beaten, bruised, and flogged beyond recognition with a cat of nine tails. He was spit upon and mocked, all by those who had hailed him as "Hosanna" when he entered Jerusalem before his death. Still, Jesus forgave. He took each stripe upon his back with all of mankind in mind. He knew He was dying for our sins, to save us, and to give us eternal life. He wanted us to know His Father as he knows Him; and the only way to the Father was through His shed blood. He could have stopped it. He could have called all of Heaven at His command to end His suffering; but instead, He chose to go to the cross. When He hung between Heaven and earth, He looked down at those mocking Him at His feet. They were laughing, telling Him to save Himself, and shredding his garments between them. Even then Jesus had compassion and forgiveness.

Luke 23:34-37 says, "And Jesus was saying, 'Father, forgive them; for they do not know what they are doing.' And they cast lots, dividing his clothes among themselves. Now the people stood by, watching; but even the rulers ridiculed and sneered at Him saying, 'He saved others [from death]; let Him save Himself if He is the Christ (the Messiah, the Anointed) of God, His Chosen One'" (AMP).

Jesus forgave everyone at the foot of the cross: those who betrayed Him, those who denied Him; those who mocked Him, and even those who crucified Him. He looked into all of eternity, and He forgave you and me. If they seek Him, He will also forgive the ones who hurt us. The stripes He

112

took on His back; each one was for your addiction, my sexual sin, for each and every thing that stands between us and God the Father. He took it for us.

SEPARATED FROM GOD

Isaiah 53:5-7 says, "But He was wounded for our transgressions, He was bruised for our iniquities; The chastisement for our peace was upon Him, And by His stripes we are healed. All we like sheep have gone astray; We have turned, everyone to his own way; And the Lord has laid on Him the iniquity of us all. He was oppressed and He was afflicted, Yet He opened not His mouth; He was led as a lamb to the slaughter..." (NKJV).

Jesus suffered for us and we were forgiven. He is the ultimate sacrifice of love and forgiveness. Imagine the pain He felt not only physically, but emotionally. At one moment before His death; as all of the past, present, and future sins of mankind were poured upon Him, His Father had to look away. I believe this was the most excruciating cry of pain that was experienced not only in all of the Bible, but all of eternity. The cry of Jesus. That gut-wrenching pain of the denial of the one who loves you the most; His Father, the One He loves, and the One who loves Him. Matthew 27:46, "About the ninth hour Jesus cried out with a loud [agonized] voice, "Eli, Eli, Lama Sabachthani?" that is, "My God, My God, Why have you forsaken Me?" (AMP).

I have heard it said that God the Father could not look upon Jesus because sin cannot exist in the presence of God. What if also for a moment God had to turn away because it hurt God the Father to see His son who had no sin, suffer with our sins? At that moment Jesus took on all of humanity's sin causing a separation between Him and His Father. Imagine that pain, that emotional pain that Jesus felt. Jesus experienced in that brief moment what an eternal separation from God's presence would feel like. I believe it was an agonizing moment of darkness and hell. He took that for us.

Jesus was perfect. He came from God the Father, and He did not have to suffer and die. He chose to experience everything that you and I would experience without Heaven, even if that meant a moment of separation from His Father. For Jesus it was a moment, but He knew for us it would be eternity.

Matthew 6:14 says, "For if you forgive other people when they sin against you, your heavenly Father will also forgive you" (NIV). We cannot take what Jesus did for us in vain. He suffered, died, and forgave all of those who hurt Him, and He forgives us. Who are we then to not forgive?

GOING THROUGH HELL

"When the centurion and those with him who were guarding Jesus
saw the earthquake and all that had happened, they were terrified,
and exclaimed, "Surely he was the Son of God!"
Matthew 27:54 (NIV)

When Jesus suffered and died on the cross, the skies went dark, the earth shook, and people ran in fear. Matthew 27:50-52, "And when Jesus had cried out again in a loud voice, he gave up his spirit. At that moment the curtain of the temple was torn in two from top to bottom. The earth shook, the rocks split, and the tombs broke open" (NIV). Did the earth quake because God His Father was angry at His Son's death; or was it the power released by Jesus' spirit?

Maybe it was both, we don't know. What we do know is that He died and on the third day He rose again. But what is known about the three days between Jesus' death and resurrection? King David prophesied the death and resurrection of Jesus Christ in Psalms 16:10 saying, "For thou wilt not leave my soul in hell; neither wilt thou suffer thine Holy One to see corruption" (KJV). We know this was about Jesus because Peter explains it again in Acts 2:27.

The book of Ephesians and 1st Peter talk about Jesus descending into the lowly parts of the earth to the realm of the dead or Hades and preaching to the "spirits in prison." Ephesians 4:9-10, "Now this, 'He *ascended*'—what does it mean but that He also *first descended* into the lower parts of the earth? He who descended is also the One who ascended far above all the heavens, that He might fill all things" (NKJV). 1 Peter 3:18-19, "For indeed Christ died for sins once for all, the Just and Righteous for the unjust and unrighteous [the Innocent for the guilty] so that He might bring us to God, having been put to death in the flesh, but made alive in the Spirit; in which He also went and preached to the spirits now in prison..." (AMP). According to these scriptures Jesus died in the flesh but was alive in the spirit. 1st Peter 3:19-20 goes on to say that Jesus preached to those who were disobedient during the time of Noah, "in which He also went and preached to the spirits now in prison, who once were disobedient, when the great patience of God was waiting in the days of Noah, during the building of the ark, in which a few, that is, eight persons [Noah's family], were brought safely through the water."

I am not a theologian by any means, I am the average lay person reading the Bible trying to figure things out. However, I think it is safe to say from reading these scriptures that after Jesus suffered and died on the cross, the earth quaked with the power of the release of His spirit. He descended to the "lowly" parts of the earth or Hades and preached to the spirits of old; and according to Revelation He holds the keys of life and death in His hands. Revelation 1:17-18, "When I saw him, I fell at his feet as though dead. Then he placed his right hand on me and said: 'Do not be afraid. I am the First and the Last. I am the Living One; I was dead, and now look, I am alive for ever and ever! And I hold the keys of death and Hades'" (NIV). Jesus came to set the captives free, both the dead and the living. Those who have gone before us, those who are living now, and those who will be born into the future if He does not return before then.

LIVING LIKE JESUS

Jesus went through hell on earth being beaten, bruised and scorned; and then according to the scriptures He descended into Hades. In other words, He literally walked through Hell. I wonder what Jesus felt when He visited that dark place of death. Jesus is compassion and life. He had to hurt for those who were already lost, those who had rejected His father long before He came to earth. If Jesus went through hell here on earth and beyond for us, what makes us think then that we won't go through hell here on earth, as well? It isn't easy to understand, especially for those who are following Him with their whole heart, except that we are no greater than Him.

Jesus took on so much for our forgiveness and yet we still sin. We walk around blindly and are deceived into doing things that will keep us from our destiny on earth. The devil doesn't care what you do whether you drink, smoke, take drugs, cuss, sell yourself, sit on a couch and do nothing, or simply indulge in a materialistic lifestyle. He really doesn't care as long as you are not seeking God and His will for your life. If he can just keep you distracted with anything, he is happy.

JESUS CARES

You might say, "you don't know what I've been through, I've been through hell." Maybe you were beaten and abused as a child, maybe you've been sexually assaulted or molested. Jesus took every pain, every hurt you have ever experienced upon his back. He took the stripes of abuse, addiction, hurt, pain, disease, murder, every pain we can think of, He took it. Every stripe, every crack of the whip that tore his flesh was for the very thing that you are holding onto that hurt you. Isaiah 53:4-6 says, "Surely He has borne our griefs and carried our sorrows; Yet we esteemed Him stricken, smitten by God, and afflicted. But He was wounded for our transgressions, He was bruised for our iniquities; the chastisement for our peace was upon Him, and by His stripes we are healed. All we like sheep have gone astray; We have turned, every one, to his own way; And the Lord has laid on Him the iniquity of us all" (NKJV).

Jesus knows what you have been through, and He cares. If He didn't, He would not have suffered the death that He did; bearing the weight of our pain upon His back. Keeping us at the forefront of his mind brought him victory over death and the grave. Not only did he have the victory, but he forgave. He forgave those who beat him, who betrayed him, who spit on him and called him names. Those who shoved his broken body and pierced his side, he forgave them all.

The Bible says in Matthew 5:45, "For he gives his sunlight to both the evil and the good, and he sends rain on the just and the unjust alike" (NLT). He gives food, sunlight and forgiveness to those who have hurt us. After all, weren't we once one of them? Didn't we once turn away from God? Are you turning away from God or are you turning to him? He's there waiting to forgive you and the ones who hurt you. Forgiving does not mean you have to allow someone who hurt you back into your life. Set boundaries and don't allow people who have not changed to hurt you again. Unless there is a criminal reason for punishment, don't expect the people that hurt you to be punished. Forgive even though that person may not have apologized or may not see the error of their ways.

Holding on to the past is like playing in the dirt. What do you have to gain by staying in the dirt pile except to get dirty? Get up and dust off. Don't let the hurt hold you down and keep you in a dirty place any longer. Forgive, pray, and move forward up the mountain to the other side to see your promises. Jesus holds the victory; the keys of life and death are in His hands. Ask Him into your heart right now and receive the gift of what He has done for you. Ask Him for the help that you need to forgive those who have hurt you and allow His transformation power to enter your life.

Chapter 7
STUDY GUIDE

REFLECT Are you harboring hatred in your heart toward someone who has hurt you?

Are you punishing that person by not forgiving them or are you really hurting yourself by carrying that pain?

Do you realize that you can pass on a root of unforgiveness and bitterness to those around you?

Do you understand that forgiving does not mean you have to allow the person who hurt you back into your life, especially if they have not changed?

READ Hebrews 12:15 "See to it that no one falls short of the grace of God and that no bitter root grows up to cause trouble and defile many."

Colossians 3:13 "Bear with each other and forgive one another if any of you has a grievance against someone. Forgive as the Lord forgave you."

Matthew 6:14 "For if you forgive other people when they sin against you, your heavenly Father will also forgive you."

DECLARE I will not carry the burden of unforgiveness any longer. It is not God's will that I carry this weight and allow roots of bitterness to entangle my heart. I will forgive with the power of Jesus, by praying and reading His word. I refuse to allow the pain of my past and the hurt inflicted on me by others to rule my life or my decisions any longer. I will allow Jesus to set me free!

PRAY Lord Jesus, I do not want to carry this burden of unforgiveness in my heart any longer. I give it to you. Please forgive me for not offering the forgiveness that you died for on the cross to _____. Help me to forgive them, even if it is a long process. I trust you to walk me through this. I do not want to pass this burden onto anyone around me. I ask you to take it from me and to help me. Thank you for forgiving me today, and I ask you to remove any root of bitterness that has tried to entangle me. Thank you for setting me free! In Jesus' name I pray. Amen!

Chapter 8
FORGETTING WHAT LIES BEHIND

"Brothers and sisters, I do not consider
that I have made it my own yet, but one thing I do:
forgetting what lies behind and reaching forward to what lies ahead"
Philippians 3:13 (AMP)

Jesus calls us not only to forgive others but also to forgive ourselves. Focusing on the things that we have done wrong in the past leaves us not only feeling guilty and condemned, but brings shame, discouragement, and depression; all of which affect our future. Romans 8:1-2 says, "Therefore, there is now no condemnation for those who are in Christ Jesus, because through Christ Jesus the law of the Spirit who gives life has set you free from the law of sin and death" (NIV). When we come to Christ and seek forgiveness, He forgives us and removes the burden of our past. He remembers it no more. However, we have human minds, and we remember. We must remind ourselves that if Jesus died on the cross, resurrected from the grave, and went to Heaven for the forgiveness of our sins; then we are forgiven. He has removed the burden of the past from us. It is no longer ours to carry, it is given to Him. When we live constantly dwelling on the past, we cannot completely move forward and become all that Christ has created us to be.

FROM MY MESS TO HIS MASTERPIECE

A PILLAR OF SALT

In the book of Genesis, the city of Sodom had fallen into such sin and depravity that there was no turning back. In all the city, God could find only Lot, Abraham's nephew, and his family who still worshiped Him. Everyone else had fallen to worship pagan gods and into deep sexual sin. God warned Lot to take his family and leave the city before it was destroyed. God sent Angels of the Lord who gave specific instructions to Lot to leave the city and not to look back.

Genesis 19:17, "When they had brought them outside, one [of the angels] said, 'Escape for your life! Do not look behind you or stop anywhere in the entire valley; escape to the mountains [of Moab], or you will be consumed and swept away'" (AMP). The angel told them not to look back, but Lot's wife, Sara, did not listen.

Genesis 19:24-26, "Then the Lord rained down brimstone (flaming sulfur) and fire on Sodom and on Gomorrah from the Lord out of heaven, and He overthrew (demolished, ended) those cities, and the entire valley, and all the inhabitants of the cities, and whatever grew on the ground. But Lot's wife, from behind him, [foolishly, longingly] looked [back toward Sodom in an act of disobedience], and she became a pillar of salt" (AMP).

Sara looked back and was turned into a pillar of salt. I don't know the significance or why God chose to turn Sara into a pillar of salt, but I do know that looking back at the past will paralyze you. I think Sara is a perfect picture of how we can look at our past and not move on. It says she looked back "longingly." Just as Sara did, we can look back and long for what was; even if what we are longing for was not good for us. After my divorce I looked back for a moment and longed for a marriage that did not work. God was freeing me from the past. I needed to move forward and not look back. Had I gone back my life would have faced certain destruction. I would not be where I am today in my relationship with Christ.

When God frees you from your past, He has better things planned for you. He calls you into a new future with hope. You cannot see your future when you are looking behind you. Our goal is to press forward, to be Christlike, and model his character in our lives. Philippians 3:13-14 says, "Brothers and Sisters I do not consider that I have made it my own yet; but one thing I do: forgetting what lies behind and reaching forward to what lies ahead, I press on toward the goal to win the [heavenly] prize of the upward call of God in Christ Jesus" (AMP).

We will never be just like Christ, but we can be Christlike, a reflection of Him. In doing so He gives us hope, He forgives our past, and helps us to forget what was behind and look forward to what is ahead. Giving your life completely and fully to Jesus breaks the chains of the past from your life. This is part of His finished work on the cross: freeing us from our sins and helping us change our ways to become more like Him.

GETTING BACK ON SOLID GROUND

I carried the burden of my abortion for many years. I could not think about it and when I did, I would shake it off. Remembering brought too much pain and forgiving myself was not an option. When God began to deal with me about forgiving myself, I told Him that I just could not do it. I knew I had to face this to move forward, but it was too hard. God reminded me that He forgave me and asked me, "Are you greater than Me? Are you the judge of your own sins?" The answer, of course, was no. God then asked me, "If I forgave you, then who are you not to forgive yourself?" In that moment I realized that I was putting myself in the place of God. I was in God's seat judging myself. That is not where I belonged, nor where I wanted to be. I asked God to forgive me, and I was able to forgive myself. I was set free from the burden that I was carrying!

If you have sought God for His forgiveness, He forgives you. Don't look to the past anymore, it is gone. Psalms 40:2 says, "He lifted me out of the slimy pit, out of the mud and mire; he set my feet on a rock and gave me a firm place to stand" (NIV). Allowing Jesus to lift us up out of the pit of our past and our wrong thinking sets our feet on solid ground. We no longer slip and slide through the mud back into our old ways. We want nothing more than to please Him and to move forward. In doing so, we experience the blessing of life and peace. Philippians 4:6-7 says that if we

You cannot
see your future
when you are
looking behind you.

@joygrantofficial
#frommymesstohismasterpiece

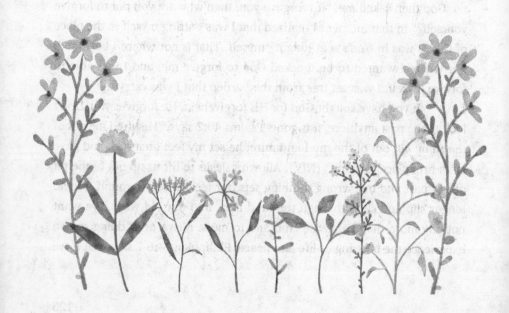

pray and look to God he will give us peace that passes all understanding, "Be anxious for nothing, but in everything by prayer and supplication, with thanksgiving, let your requests be made known to God; and the peace of God, which surpasses all understanding, will guard your hearts and minds through Christ Jesus" (NKJV).

Now, I can find myself in the most unpredictable place in life and still have peace! I seek Him daily and I want nothing more than His perfect will for my life. There is no losing when you give your life completely over to Him, only winning and joy.

THE "NO" OF YESTERDAY

"I can do all things through Christ who strengthens me."
Philippians 4:13 (KJV)

I cared for my mother until she passed away in 2018. She was the joy of our family. In the dark times of our childhood, she was the light that made us smile. When my dad was not home, she was happy and funny; but when he would come home, she was quiet and sad.

I was sitting with my mother one evening before she passed away. I saw a bug on the floor and tried to hit it with my shoe. Instead of hitting the bug, I hit my finger and jammed the joint; it was swollen and bruised. When I showed it to my mother, she raised her right hand and showed me her finger. It was crooked between the knuckle and her nail. It looked as though it had been broken and had not healed properly. As I asked her what happened a memory suddenly flashed through my mind. She answered, "I got it caught in a car door." Immediately my stomach cringed as my mind took me back to that night.

I was raised seeing blood, listening to fighting and watching my mother cover her black eyes with makeup. That night was particularly bad, the fight carried outside, down the stairs into the alley where my father parked his car. My sister and I watched from the window of our third-floor Chicago apartment. My mother was crying as she followed my father down the stairs and into the dark where he got into his car. She tried to stop him, but he slammed the door on her hand and drove off. I remember the blood curdling scream. My sister and I ran down to help her.

I WANT TO DO BETTER

That is how we were raised; these are our childhood memories. There was no guidance or direction given in our young lives. It is really kind of odd looking back at the type of child I was. I always wanted to do better, and it is still a God given desire inside of me. I liked to draw and get good grades. I tried to make my parents proud of me, to notice me. I often tried to do good, productive things on my own. I had a friend who was a Girl Scout; I admired her patches, she seemed to be having so much fun. I asked my mother if I could join, but for whatever reason she said no. I would ride public transportation with another friend to the Art Institute of Chicago. I was about ten. It still surprises me that I took public transportation with another child and no adult. My friend took art classes at the museum, and I would sit and wait for her in the hallway. Sometimes I would walk through the museum amazed at the artwork. I asked if I could take the classes with her. I don't know why, but the answer was no.

Finally, the same friend who was a Girl Scout was also in a dance class at our neighborhood park. Again, when I asked if I could join and be in the performance, the answer was no. We could not afford it. The instructor of the class felt sorry for me and let me practice the dance with them anyway. When it was time for the actual performance, I asked for the money to buy the costume but was told that we could not afford it. When I told the teacher that I could not buy the costume she said, "that's okay you can dance anyway."

The evening of the performance I stayed in the back refusing to go out without a costume. I was embarrassed; but the teacher talked me into dancing with the girls just as I was, so I did. I don't remember exactly what I was wearing, but it was just my regular street clothes. When I began dancing with the other girls the audience laughed at me, I guess because I looked so out of place. I ran off the stage. That was the last time I tried to do something on my own as a child. Something inside of me gave up.

I don't blame my mother for this. I am sure that she was struggling financially and had her reasons for saying no; but the discouragement of hearing "no you can't" has followed me most of my life. I now know that the discouraging voice is not God, but it is a voice that I fight.

GOD'S "YES" OF TODAY

The "no" of yesterday does not stop God's yes today. In 2013 I learned of a ministry called Out of Darkness that reaches women who are exploited in the streets of Atlanta. I wanted my church to become involved and connected. I didn't know who to go to or who to talk to, my church seemed huge to me. I felt insignificant to the size of it; but God led me to speak to the connections pastor of our church. I remember as I sat and talked with him about the ministry, I was sure that he would see the importance and significance of their work and give them a call. I want to laugh out loud here because that is not at all what happened. Without a thought, he opened his laptop and said, "So what do you want to call *your* group?" Stunned, I panicked inside, "My group?" "Yes, your group." He began typing away and said, "We'll just call it 'Joy Grant's Group' until you come up with a name." I left the church shocked and rejoicing at the same time, and for three years afterwards I was able to lead a group of volunteers to Atlanta every Friday night to minister in the streets with the Atlanta Dream Center and Out of Darkness. When I moved from the area, I passed the torch to a trusted friend in the group who kept the volunteers going.

GOD NEEDS YOU TO FULFILL YOUR DESTINY

Don't let negative and discouraging thoughts continue to control your life. Believe that you are strong enough in Christ to change your way of thinking, no matter how the negative thoughts got there. Begin reading the scripture and realize who you are in Christ. God has put gifts and talents within you that no one else has; and He needs you to realize and believe this so that you can fulfill your destiny here on earth. According to Ephesians 2:10, "You are God's workmanship, created in Christ Jesus for good works." There is a plan and a purpose for each one of us, we need only to seek Him to find out what that plan is. When you give your life to Jesus the no of yesterday is gone, and your future is full of hope and good things.

Hope and vision keep us moving forward and excited. It gives us goals, and without it we become stagnant. Proverbs 29:10 says, "Where there is no vision, the people perish: but he that keepeth the law, happy is he" (KJV). I am the happiest when I have a goal to reach and that is because God put that desire in me. He has put desires in you, too. How exciting is it to know that there is so much hope and future for us? We have it in Christ! God has good things in store for us and He wants to bless us. Matthew 7:11 says, "If you then, being evil, know how to give good gifts to your children, how much more will your Father who is in heaven give good things to those who ask Him!" (NIV).

THY WILL BE DONE ON EARTH AS IT IS IN HEAVEN
If you are not sure how to seek God's will for your life, I have a simple answer. I do it every day. I pray part of the Lord's prayer from Matthew 6:10, "Thy will be done on earth, as it is in heaven" (NKJV). This tells me that there is a specific will for my life in Heaven and I am asking God to bring that will for my life down to earth. Whatever that will is that He has for me, I am asking Him to make it happen here on earth. You can do that, too. This causes us to walk in faith and in hope, knowing that He has a perfect will for us and something great planned for us. It keeps our eyes on Him and causes us to want to please Him, as He is our Heavenly Father.

It takes the pressure off of ourselves and puts our trust solely in Him. Corinthians 5:21 says, "God made him who had no sin to be sin for us, so that in Him we might become the righteousness of God" (NIV). Once we accept Jesus as our Lord and Savior, we become the righteousness of Christ. We are children of the Most-High King. This means we are royalty!

BROKEN CHAINS

"At once all the prison doors flew open,
and everyone's chains came loose."
Acts 16:26 (NIV)

As I said earlier, I struggled with discouragement. Do I still struggle with discouragement? Yes, but I have learned not to focus on my feelings; but on the word of God and that His promises are faithful and true. God promises in Hebrews 13:5 to never leave us nor forsake us, and in Psalms 138:8 He promises to accomplish what He says He will do.

Discouragement comes in many ways; and if we allow it to go on, it will take away valuable time and energy from our lives. One day as I was praying, I asked God to take the discouragement away from me. God told me that He had already broken the chains of discouragement off my life, and I am the one picking up the chains. All at once I saw a picture of myself picking up heavy, broken chains that were lying on the ground and carrying them over my shoulder. I realized in that moment that the chains of discouragement were no longer binding me or holding me down. They were already broken, all I had to do is lay them back down and walk away.

DO YOU BELIEVE IT?

Sometimes we don't realize that we have already been set free from what we are struggling with. When you ask in Jesus' Name to be set free from discouragement, anxiety, depression, addiction, self-hatred, greed, envy or whatever it is that you are struggling with, Jesus breaks the chains without hesitation. Matthew 7:7 says, "Ask, and it will be given to you; seek, and you will find; knock, and it will be opened to you;" (NIV) and John 14:13 says, "And whatever you ask in My name, that I will do, that the Father may be glorified in the Son. If you ask anything in My name, I will do it" (NKJV). Whatever we ask in His name that is according to His will is done. It is up to us to believe it. My chains of discouragement are broken, your chains that weigh you down are broken. Do we still have work to do to overcome these things? Yes. We may have to do tangible things such as get a job, continue with our therapies, or even seek therapy if it is needed.

I can honestly say at this moment of my life, I am fighting discouragement again. We recently have gone through some traumatic events as a family, and I am still working on this book. I know that I have to continue forward and seek God; but the thought of taking the steps to find a publisher and go through a process that I am not familiar with is overwhelming. I must take the steps to fight through the discouragement and move forward through my actions, and through seeking Him and reading His word. God promises to finish what He has started, as it says in Philippians 1:6, He is faithful to complete the work in us.

PAUL AND SILAS SET FREE

In the Book of Acts, Paul and Silas were unjustly put in prison for delivering a woman from her demons. While in chains, instead of becoming discouraged and complaining about their circumstances, they began singing and praising God; and God delivered them. Acts 16:25-27, "Around midnight Paul and Silas were praying and singing hymns to God, and the other prisoners were listening. Suddenly, there was a massive earthquake, and the prison was shaken to its foundations. All the doors immediately flew open, and the chains of every prisoner fell off! The jailer woke up to see the prison doors wide open" (NLT).

Paul and Silas were set free by their praises to God. They were in chains, and their chains fell off, they were broken. What if Paul and Silas took their chains with them when they were released from prison by God? What a silly thought, but that is basically what we are doing when we go back to what God has already delivered us from.

We can keep ourselves in chains by condemning ourselves for our mistakes and focusing on what is wrong in life; or we can believe that Jesus has set us free and made a way for us where there seems to be no way. Isaiah 43:18-19 says, "Do not remember the former things, nor consider the things of old. Behold, I will do a new thing, now it shall spring forth; Shall you not know it? I will even make a road in the wilderness and rivers in the desert" (NKJV). Genesis 35:3 says that God will answer us in our distress, "Then come, let us go up to Bethel, where I will build an altar to God, who answered me in the day of my distress and who has been with me wherever I have gone" (NIV).

We can praise God in the midst of our trials and circumstances; and as David did in the Book of Samuel, encourage ourselves in the Lord. 1 Samuel 30:6, "And David was greatly distressed; for the people spake of stoning him, because the soul of all the people was grieved, every man for his sons and for his daughters: but David encouraged himself in the Lord his God" (NKJV). We can believe that He has greater plans for us and watch our chains fall to the ground. We don't have to wait for someone to recognize how well we are doing or seek others' approval.

Isaiah 9:4 says, "For God will break the chains that bind his people and the whip that scourges them..." (TLB) and Psalms 107:10-16 says, "Some sat in darkness, in utter darkness, prisoners suffering in iron chains, because they rebelled against God's commands and despised the plans of the Most-High. So, he subjected them to bitter labor; they stumbled, and there was no one to help. Then they cried to the Lord in their trouble, and he saved them from their distress. He brought them out of darkness, the utter darkness, and broke away their chains. Let them give thanks to the Lord for his unfailing love and his wonderful deeds for mankind, for he breaks down gates of bronze and cuts through bars of iron" (NIV). This scripture ends in praise and thankfulness. We once were bound but now we are free. You are no longer in the chains that held you down; Christ has set you free.

EXPOSED AGAIN

Are you picking up the chains of the past? Once we ask Christ for deliverance, we are set free. Some things may take time, and we may have to work hard to overcome them; but when faced with the choice we can remember that we are free. Would someone who has been released from prison choose to go back and be chained?

When we go back to our previous sins, we throw off God's blanket of grace and we are exposed to the enemy again. We are naked and vulnerable, but God has given us a way of escape. 1 Corinthians 10:13 says, "The temptations in your life are no different from what others experience. And God is faithful. He will not allow the temptation to be more than you can stand. When you are tempted, he will show you a way out so that you can endure" (NLT). Knowing this, that God will make a way of escape for you, don't purposely go back to the things of the past. In order to go back to the past, you will have to refuse God's word that you have already learned.

When you ignore God, your heart will become hard towards Him. Hebrews 3:7-8 says, "Therefore, as the Holy Spirit says: 'Today, if you hear His voice, do not harden your hearts, as you did in the rebellion...'" (NIV). In other words, when you are tempted to "rebel" don't refuse God and allow your heart to become hard towards Him. Hardening of heart is considered rebellion, but God has made a way of escape for you. He has already delivered you and set you free.

A DEAD SNAKE CAN STILL STRIKE

Going back to a place of sin is like reaching down to touch the head of a dead snake. A dead snake can still bite you. One day my ex and I ran over a poisonous copperhead snake. We had got out of the truck to see it because it was so large, and I thought it would be okay to reach down and pick it up. I don't know why I wanted to do this, but as I did my ex yelled at me to stop. He told me a dead snake can still bite. I looked this up and found this interesting fact on the National Geographic website, "By the time the snake has lost its head, it's dead and the basic body functions have ceased, but there is still some reflexive action. In other words, snakes have the capability of biting and injecting venom even after the head has been severed, even though it is dead."[2] Just like reaching down for that snake, be careful about going back to dangerous situations, it can still strike you. God has given you the strength and power through His word to resist as it says in James 4:7, "Submit yourselves, then, to God. Resist the devil, and he will flee from you" (NIV).

CAST YOUR CARES AND TEMPTATIONS ON CHRIST!

You might be reading this and literally sitting in prison. Not only are you in the chains of your past mistakes, but you are locked away from society. Whatever the reason may be that you are there, remember this, God loves you and He wants to set you free. The Bible is full of examples of those God delivered and set free. Paul was physically released from prison; Daniel was thrown to the lions' den for praying to God instead of the king, but the lions did not touch him; Shadrach, Meshach, and Abed-Nego were thrown to the furnace for refusing to worship a golden idol and came out without the smell of smoke; Joseph and the coat of many colors was wrongly accused and put into prison but came out elevated to royalty in the government of Egypt; these are just a few. You, too, can be delivered. Maybe it will take time to actually be released from where you are physically, but you can be instantly delivered spiritually and begin to see miracles unfold in your life.

You don't have to pick up the broken chains anymore. Cast your cares and temptations on Jesus! He promises in Matthew 11:28-30 that He will carry them for you, "Come to me, all you who are weary and burdened, and I will give you rest. Take my yoke upon you and learn from me, for I am gentle and humble in heart, and you will find rest for your souls. For my yoke is easy and my burden is light" (NIV). What a great God we serve who loves us enough to do this for us. Whether bound physically, spiritually, or emotionally we can be set free!

Chapter 8
STUDY GUIDE

REFLECT Do you carry the weight and burden of your past mistakes by blaming and beating yourself up?

Sometimes the most difficult thing to do is forgive ourselves. Can you release those burdens to Jesus without looking back to pick them up again?

Do you believe that Jesus has an exciting future planned for you?

What is the one thing that you would love to do to serve and honor Jesus?

READ Philippians 3:13 "Brothers and sisters, I do not consider that I have made it my own yet, but one thing I do: forgetting what lies behind and reaching forward to what lies ahead."

Romans 8:1-2 "Therefore, there is now no condemnation for those who are in Christ Jesus, because through Christ Jesus the law of the Spirit who gives life has set you free from the law of sin and death."

Psalms 40:2 "He lifted me out of the slimy pit, out of the mud and mire; he set my feet on a rock and gave me a firm place to stand."

Matthew 11:28-30 "Come to me, all you who are weary and burdened, and I will give you rest. Take my yoke upon you and learn from me, for I am gentle and humble in heart, and you will find rest for your souls. For my yoke is easy and my burden is light."

Proverbs 29:10 "Where there is no vision, the people perish: but he that keepeth the law, happy is he."

DECLARE I am created by God for a plan and a purpose. God puts dreams and visions into my heart, and I was meant to fulfill them. I am here for a reason. I am forgiven by God for my past; He sees it no more. I will focus on my future with Him and not look behind. I will forgive myself as He has forgiven me. I cannot wait to begin to serve Him and experience the joy it will bring!

PRAY Jesus, thank you so much for your finished work on the cross. You died for me, for my sins, and to give me a future and hope. I am sorry for holding onto my past mistakes, things that You have already forgiven me for and forgotten about! I put my life and my spirit into your hands, and I ask you to give me a new and exciting vision of my future. When the temptation comes to look behind, I will remember what you did for me and look forward. Thank you for loving me! In Jesus' name I pray. Amen!

WORTHY

*"But God, being rich in mercy, because of the great love
with which he loved us even when we were dead in our trespasses,
made us alive together with Christ— by grace you have been saved."*
Ephesians 2:4-5 (ESV)

Worthy. It is not a word we often use to describe ourselves. We think of Jesus as worthy. As Christians, we sing songs of praise such as "Worthy is the lamb" and "Thou art worthy." The fact is, Jesus *is* worthy; we love Him, we worship Him, we adore Him.

But what does Jesus think about us? Are we worthy to stand in His presence? Throughout the Bible you find those who kneel in the presence of God. Are we worthy to even untie His shoes? John the Baptist said of Jesus in John 1:27, "He is the one who comes after me, the straps of whose sandals I am not worthy to untie" (NIV). Are we worthy of His love, of His sacrifice for us or the good things He has in store for us? The answer to all of these questions is yes! This can be so hard to believe. Do we really know who we are in Christ and who He has created us to be? Do we believe the good things He says about us, or do we allow the thoughts that control our mind to dominate our existence and our destiny?

You may not feel as though your heart is pure or your hands are clean. You may be feeling unworthy, not good enough to love or be loved by God; but that is *not* how *God feels* towards you. Most of us, Christian and non-Christian alike, do not believe that we are worthy of the good things of God. We may say we are; we may even think we are, but we often do not live like we are. We don't live up to the potential of the talents, the callings, the creativity that God has put in us; and we see ourselves in the hazy rear-view mirror of our past. We compare ourselves to others around us and look to them for affirmation; and when we don't receive it, we feel bad about ourselves. We secretly, and sometimes unknowingly, shy away from places and events that surround us with people who we think are "better" than us. Subconsciously and sometimes unknowingly, I was only allowing myself to achieve or be in situations that I thought I was "worthy" of.

A LIFELONG PROCESS

My sense of unworthiness kept me trapped in a vicious cycle of allowing myself to be used in relationships and from reaching my highest potential in Christ. 1 Corinthians 2:9 says, "Eye has not seen, nor ear heard, nor have entered into the heart of man, the things God has prepared for those who love Him" (NKJV). If this is true, that He has such good things in store for us, then why do we find ourselves thinking we are just not good enough? Past mistakes and wrong beliefs kept me trapped, but I won't allow that any longer. Jesus has opened my eyes to how much He loves me and how much He wants for me. He wants to open your eyes, too.

Romans 12:2 says, "Do not conform to the pattern of this world, but be transformed by the renewing of your mind. Then you will be able to test and approve what God's will is--his good, pleasing and perfect will" (NIV). I have found the "renewing" of my mind to be the biggest challenge of my life. I read that scripture for the first time when I was twenty-five years old. Initially I thought that if I could forgive my father, my mind would be renewed. Through prayer and counseling, I worked through forgiving him. I soon found out that was only the beginning and there was much more work to do. Renewing my mind has been an ongoing and lifelong process.

MELTED, SMASHED-UP AND USED

In my twenties I was trying hard to get my life together, working full time and raising my two daughters alone. I wanted my girls in Sunday school, so I joined a very small church. While there, I attended a class that the pastor's wife decided to teach on being sexually pure. Meaning well, she gave an analogy on purity and what men want. She said that men do not want girls who are "used;" giving an example of having a melted, smashed candy bar as opposed to a fresh, new candy bar. "Which one would you want?" she asked. "Do you want the smashed, melted candy bar or the new candy bar? Men don't want 'used' girls; they want the 'new' candy bar." I felt like the most "impure" of the group. I was embarrassed and appalled. I felt awful, ashamed, and almost dirty.

I was disturbed and saddened as I tried to absorb this twisted idea of who I was in the eyes of God. Not only was I a single mom, but I had given a child up for adoption *and* had an abortion. So, I was really "melted, smashed up, and used." Who would want me? According to the pastor's wife, no one.

SAME WORDS, DIFFERENT PEOPLE

I was able to tell her how her analogy hurt me, and that I did not think it was a good example to use for girls. Girls like me, I am "that girl." The girl that everyone wants to know what has become of her; not because they care, but because they are curious. The girl who got pregnant twice in high school. I was the girl that was used as a "bad example" in our family. It was said right in front of me, "You don't want to grow up to be like Joy, do you?" In other words, pregnant, single and alone. I already felt worthless in the eyes of any man, so to hear this from church leaders and family members left scars. The most ironic thing is when I was finally married, one of the favorite things my ex-husband would say to me was, "I'm the only one who would marry you." In other words, "no one else wanted you." It was much later in life when I realized how much statements like these hurt my self-worth and my spirit deep inside.

However, something I have learned both in my life and in listening to others is: the enemy is not creative. The enemy knows how to carry on a theme of words against you; even if those words are from different people, with years in between them. The patterns of abuse, the behaviors of the abusers, and the tricks of the enemy all are the same.

SOMETHING WAS MISSING

Years had passed and I was in my forties. I had been through a marriage full of abuse and a terrible divorce, and I was completely sold out and devoted to Jesus. I did not want to make the same mistakes again. I was now surrounded by good friends, wonderful children, a great church and had made a new life for myself. But I still had something missing deep inside. There was a deep loneliness that I just could not shake no matter how hard I tried. I organized singles groups and women's groups with many events and outings.

I even became a ministry leader within my church. I was constantly surrounded by friends and activities, but still something was missing. I was excited to get up and go to church every week; but just like that, one Sunday I couldn't go. I had hit another wall that I could not break through.

Suddenly, out of nowhere I felt alone, different, not like everyone else around me. I was surrounded by beautiful families and couples, with what I imagined were perfect lives, beautiful homes, cars, and great jobs. Here I was again only this time in my forties and divorced, alone, living in an apartment, having lost almost everything, even my job and starting over from scratch. I could not understand where these feelings were coming from. We were happy. We loved the area we were living in, God was blessing us and we were attending the most fantastic church pretty much anywhere in the world. But out of nowhere I wasn't able to get up and go.

I was ashamed, I didn't feel good enough. I was lonely. I fought through these feelings most Sundays, but just walking into church was difficult for me. Some days I would give into the feelings and stay home, especially when my son was with his father. It was just too hard to walk into church alone. Sound familiar? The same thing that happened in my thirties when I met my ex-husband was happening again in my forties. But this time it was different. When I began to experience these feelings again, I remembered having gone through this before and the trap that was set for me. I did not want that again; and so, this time instead of running to a man, I ran to Jesus.

"GOD, HELP ME!"

One Sunday morning I couldn't take it anymore. I was alone and had gotten dressed for church, but I couldn't even bring myself to walk out of the front door. The feelings of loneliness and inadequacy overtook me. I was anguished and I fell to my knees in my dining room begging God for an answer and to help me. As I prayed, I could feel the presence of Jesus fill the room as though He were standing right in front of me. My eyes were closed, but I could see His feet. I began to weep. I heard a loud voice in my spirit say, "stand up." I stood up, still praying and weeping. In my spirit I could see the face of Jesus, and I cried. He said, "touch my face" and it was as though I could actually feel His beard in my hands. And He said to me, "say this: 'I am worthy.'" I was so confused; I couldn't comprehend this. I shook my head and thought, "I am worthy? You are worthy, God, not me." I heard it again, "say this: 'I am worthy.'" Again, I argued in my spirit, "that is not what we say; we say, 'thou art worthy!'" God is worthy, not me.

Then Jesus said it louder in my spirit, "I am telling you to say you are worthy. You are worthy of my love. You are worthy of my dying for you on the cross. I came for you, and if you were the only one on earth, I would come for you and die for you again. You are worthy."

At hearing this I fell back to the floor and just worshiped Him. I could not stop weeping and praising Him. I felt just like the woman at the well in the Book of John. I finally understood that I was worthy of His love, and how much He loves me. I am worthy. I am worthy of His love. Since that day I have never walked into a church looking down. I walk in with my head held high, hearing I am worthy, I am worthy of HIS LOVE. I finally understand that I deserve the blessings that God has in store for me; not because I did anything to earn them, but because I am a child

Jesus doesn't see
a bad example.

He sees beauty,
potential and who
He created us
to be.

of the King. We are the children of God deserving of His love as it says in 1 John 3:1, "See what great love the Father has lavished on us, that we should be called children of God! And that is what we are!" (NIV). Jesus doesn't see melted candy bars and bad examples. He sees beauty, potential, and who He created us to be.

WE ARE A ROYAL PRIESTHOOD

How many people are afraid to go to church alone? Maybe that's you right now. Don't let the enemy tell you that you aren't worth it anymore. YOU ARE WORTHY OF HIS LOVE. He loves you just as you are and where you are. It doesn't matter what you have done. You may consider yourself to be the worst of the worst, but He doesn't see you that way. He sees you as He created you; and sees you with your longings to be that person that He created you to be. He knows that you have been led astray by the enemy; and He is waiting to forgive you, restore you and make you whole. Don't be afraid or ashamed, that is just another tactic of the enemy.

The enemy does not want you to think that you deserve any good thing. He wants you to believe the lies he has spoken to you. Just stop and listen. Listen to the fact that God loves YOU and ONLY YOU. Yes, only you. He loves each one of us as if we were the only one on earth, just as He told me that day in my dining room. His love is not just for some of us, it is for all of us. John 3:16 says, "For God so loved the world that he gave his one and only Son, that *whoever* believes in him shall not perish but have eternal life" (NIV). He so loved the world that He came and died for everyone, not just some.

1 Peter says we are a royal priesthood called out of darkness into His light, "But you are a chosen race, a royal priesthood, a holy nation, a people for his own possession, that you may proclaim the excellencies of him who called you out of darkness into his marvelous light." We are worth more than silver or gold, more than rubies or diamonds. He created the earth for us with water, birds, land, and air. He put the stars and the moon and sun in the sky for us. He loves us more than all of His creation. If He had to do it again, He would create it again for us. He loves each one of us that much, and He gave His life for us. Stop thinking about who you

were and start believing who you *are* in Christ. It was no surprise to God that you or I would fall or fail. But He also knew the time would come when we would get back up and do it right.

The world says you are worthless, God says you are worthy. The world says you are unlovable, God says you are loved. The world says you are unforgiveable, God says you are forgiven. The world says you are unredeemable, God says you are redeemed. The world says you are lost, God says you are found. The world says you are forsaken, God says you are saved. The world says you are alone, God says He will never leave you. The world says you are depressed, God says you are full of His joy. The world says that you are addicted and chained, God says you are set free. The world says you are dirty, God says you are washed white by the blood of the Lamb. The world says you are an orphan, God says you are sons and daughters of Christ. The world says you are weak, God says you are strong.

STOP THINKING THAT

Your past does not matter to Jesus, He died so that you can have a new life. He never gives up on us and doesn't look at us as bad examples. He sees us as His beloved children through His eyes of love. He sees His child who has gone astray, and He loves us back to life. He doesn't see used and damaged goods. He sees all that is new, and all that you can be. He has life and joy waiting for you. He wants to give you gifts. He adores you, yes even in the state you are in now. He doesn't see your present condition; He sees your heart and will make you strong in your weakness. 2 Corinthians 12:9 says, "My grace is sufficient for you, for my power is made perfect in weakness. Therefore, I will boast all the more gladly of my weaknesses, so that the power of Christ may rest upon me" (NIV). And Ephesians 2:8 says, "For by grace you have been saved through faith. And this is not your own doing; it is the gift of God" (ESV).

There is nothing that you can do to earn the love of God. It is there waiting for you, free to receive. So, stop thinking about the fall and start thinking about getting up. Put down that thing that is risking your life and relationship with God and with others, it's not worth it. God has so much more planned for you, so much better. I can tell you now that I am confident in my relationship with Him, and I would risk *nothing* in exchange for it.

Stop thinking that you are not worthy, not good enough to receive His love. Stop thinking that you are too "bad" or have gone too far. There are no bad people, only good people who have gone astray. If God does not see you as "bad," then don't see yourself as bad, but listen to His voice. We have all sinned and fallen short of His Glory. Isaiah 53:6, "All we like sheep have gone astray; We have turned, every one, to his own way; And the Lord has laid on Him the iniquity of us all." Understand your worth in Christ. You are worth far more than you ever dreamed. He loves you, He cares for you, and He wants the best for you. You are worthy of His love.

A NEW CREATION IN CHRIST

"Therefore, if anyone is in Christ, he is a new creation;
old things have passed away; behold, all things have become new."
2 Corinthians 5:17 (NKJV)

When you give your life to Jesus Christ you are stepping out of the life you were living into a new life. Jesus explains in John 3:1-8 that we are "born again" not in the body, but in the spirit: "There was a man of the Pharisees named Nicodemus, a ruler of the Jews. This man came to Jesus by night and said to Him, 'Rabbi, we know that You are a teacher come from God; for no one can do these signs that You do unless God is with him.' Jesus answered and said to him, 'Most assuredly, I say to you, unless one is born again, he cannot see the kingdom of God.' Nicodemus said to Him, 'How can a man be born when he is old? Can he enter a second time into his mother's womb and be born?' Jesus answered, 'Most assuredly, I say to you, unless one is born of water and the Spirit, he cannot enter the kingdom of God. That which is born of the flesh is flesh, and that which is born of the Spirit is spirit. Do not marvel that I said to you, 'You must be born again.' The wind blows where it wishes, and you hear the sound of it, but cannot tell where it comes from and where it goes. So is everyone who is born of the Spirit" (NKJV).

Not only are we born again in the Spirit; but we are now covered in the grace of God that forgives us of our sins, protects us, and helps us through the struggles of this life. Our struggles do not end, but we can now go to Him and find direction and peace. We are new creations and living a new life. The grace of God is like a warm blanket that surrounds us in the peace and love of God the Father, given freely to us by the shed blood of Jesus Christ.

When you give your life completely to Christ you not only feel changed, but you are excited and free. 2 Corinthians 5:17 says, "Therefore, if anyone is in Christ, he is a new creation; old things have passed away; behold, all things have become new." However, don't be surprised when the friends you hung around with or even family members don't believe in your new life or that you have changed. They might not understand and may even laugh at you. If you were a drug addict, they may still see you as an addict and might even tempt you to do the drugs again. If you lived a certain lifestyle and still have the same friends, don't be surprised when they are calling you to go back to the lifestyle you have left or are trying to leave.

THE ACCUSERS – THOSE CLOSEST TO YOU

Satan is called the accuser of the brethren and he doesn't want you to change or to succeed. The Bible says in Revelation that Satan accuses us before God both day and night. Revelation 12:9-10, "So the great dragon was cast out, that serpent of old, called the Devil and Satan, who deceives the whole world; he was cast to the earth, and his angels were cast out with him. Then I heard a loud voice saying in heaven, 'Now salvation, and strength, and the kingdom of our God, and the power of His Christ have come, for the accuser of our brethren, who accused them before our God day and night, has been cast down'" (NKJV).

Sometimes Satan will come to accuse you of your past through the people who know you the best. Other times, you will accuse yourself by carrying your own guilt and shame, allowing it to weigh you down. When you give your life to Jesus remember that the old person you were (the past) is gone, and you are made new. Isaiah 43:18 says, "Remember not the former things, nor consider the things of old. Behold, I am doing a new thing; now it springs forth, do you not perceive it? I will make a way in the wilderness and rivers in the desert." And Revelations 21:5 says, "Then He who sat on the throne said, 'Behold, I make all things new'" (NKJV). This means that Jesus is continuing to make "all things" new from now until the end of time.

While writing this book I go back and review what I have already written. When I do, I feel like I am reading the story of someone else! Then I realize that I *am* reading about someone else. I am no longer the person that I was. I am a new creation in Christ. I don't think the same or have the same goals and morals that I had then. I am not floating aimlessly through life, and I have a purpose. God has a plan for me, just as He has for you. I now have a new and good foundation to stand on and though tests and trials come, it is unshakeable. But in order to gain that foundation, I had to make changes and begin walking out my new life.

Some of your friends may abandon you but don't be discouraged, seek God and His new path for your life. It may be lonely at first, but eventually those around you will begin to see the new you. You will find new friends who are like minded and believers, and the old friends may even come back. I have a friend who laughed at me when I first gave my life to Christ. She abandoned our friendship but when I caught up with her years later I found out that she had accepted Jesus into her life. Now she and her family are strong Christians.

NEW LIFE
Becoming a new creation in Christ means to put off our "old selves." Just like Lazarus when Jesus raised him from the dead, we take off our "grave clothes." John 11:44, "The dead man came out, his hands and feet wrapped with strips of linen, and a cloth around his face. Jesus said to them, 'Take off the grave clothes and let him go'" (NIV). We take off the old life, the old ways and begin a new life putting on new, clean

clothes. That is when we begin practicing good things and laying down all of the things that once took us away from God. Ephesians 4:22-24 says, "to put off your old self, which belongs to your former manner of life and is corrupt through deceitful desires, and to be renewed in the spirit of your minds, and to put on the new self, created after the likeness of God in true righteousness and holiness" (ESV).

Colossians 3:1-10 gives us good instruction on how to begin our new lives in Christ: "Since you have been raised to new life with Christ, set your sights on the realities of heaven, where Christ sits in the place of honor at God's right hand. Think about the things of heaven, not the things of earth. For you died to this life, and your real life is hidden with Christ in God. And when Christ, who is your life, is revealed to the whole world, you will share in all His glory.

So put to death the sinful, earthly things lurking within you. Have nothing to do with sexual immorality, impurity, lust, and evil desires. Don't be greedy, for a greedy person is an idolater, worshiping the things of this world. Because of these sins, the anger of God is coming. You used to do these things when your life was still part of this world. But now is the time to get rid of anger, rage, malicious behavior, slander, and dirty language. Don't lie to each other, for you have stripped off your old sinful nature and all its wicked deeds. Put on your new nature and be renewed as you learn to know your Creator and become like him" (NLT).

Keeping our minds on Christ and on the "things above," seeking His good and perfect will for your life will keep your mind and heart guarded and protected from the things of the world. Seek Him first, then all of these "things" will be added to you as it says in Matthew 6:33, "But seek first the kingdom of God and His righteousness, and all these things shall be added to you" (ESV). What is it that God will "add" to us? Good things: the fruits of the spirit of love, peace and joy. Galatians 5:22-25, "But the fruit of the Spirit is love, joy, peace, patience, kindness, goodness, faithfulness, gentleness, self-control; against such things there is no law. And those who belong to Christ Jesus have crucified the flesh with its passions and desires. If we live by the Spirit, let us also keep in step with the Spirit" (ESV).

I no longer identify with the woman who I was; but I live knowing that God will fulfill my every need and desire. God has greater plans for us than we could ever imagine or think. I know this because He says so in His word, and His word is true and full of promises. His word gives us hope and keeps us moving forward toward the goal.

THE OLD HAS PASSED AWAY, ALL THINGS HAVE BECOME NEW

If you have accepted Jesus into your heart as your Lord and your Savior, you are a new creation, the old has passed away, all things have become new. You can forget what is behind and press forward toward His perfect will for your life, knowing that He will provide for every need and fulfill your every desire. His plans and purposes will become your desire as you seek Him. Not only will He meet your needs, but He will do as the scripture says, superabundantly more than all that we dare ask or think beyond our greatest prayers, hopes, or dreams. Walk in faith, seeking Him continually and never give up.

Isaiah 65:17 says, "For behold, I create new heavens and a new earth; And the former shall not be remembered or come to mind" (NKJV). He takes all that was old and makes it new. That is everything you ever did, said, or wanted to do that was against the will of God is gone. It is forgotten. You are made new. Follow Him and you will see His goodness towards you!

THE RIVER OF LIFE

"And he showed me a pure river of water of life, clear as crystal, proceeding from the throne of God and of the Lamb."
Revelation 22:1 (NKJV)

As you begin to allow God to renew your mind, be careful who you listen to, what you see, and what you fill your mind with. What we take in with our eyes and who we listen to is critical to how we think and who we become. Again, as Proverbs 23:7 says, our thoughts give birth and life to our actions. When we think good things, we act on good things. And

149

so, the opposite can happen, when we think and dwell on negative or bad thoughts, our actions can be negative or bad. For instance, if you're struggling with depression, you might be tempted to feed your sadness with depressing tv shows, with overeating, or with the temporary high of overspending on shopping. Worse yet, maybe with the temporary high of drugs or alcohol. If you are lonely, you might be tempted to call your ex or the person who you know you should stay away from.

Sometimes when we are struggling to change and are tempted, we seek justification and surround ourselves with the people who we know will agree with us. This is called "fleeing to the itching of the ear" in the Bible. In other words, instead of seeking out sound advice, we enjoy hearing from someone who will pacify us and tell us that what we are doing is okay. After waiting on God for eleven years and then meeting my ex-husband, I cannot tell you how many people told me that I "deserved" to go out with him; that I had waited long enough for someone to come into my life. While these words may have been true to a certain extent, they were not sound advice from God. Sound advice would have been, wait and get to know him, be cautious and pray. You may be hearing that you "deserve" to go party and get drunk, after all you worked hard all week; when sound advice would be, no, don't risk the DUI. Or maybe, you "deserve" to go and splurge on that large purchase; when really, sound advice would be to pay your past due bills.

WRONG AFFIRMATION

This applies to the church, as well. You can find a church where you feel comfortable and accepted, but it doesn't convict you to change or to grow. God wants you to grow, He wants you to change, and He always wants it for the better. If you are in a church that doesn't love you enough to see the best for you, to see you change and become all that Christ calls you to be, keep looking until you find it. You are going to do the hard work Monday through Sunday between yourself and God, but a church should also be encouraging you in the direction that God is leading you.

2 Timothy 4:3-4 says, "For the time will come when people will not put up with sound doctrine. Instead, to suit their own desires, they

As you begin
to allow God to
renew your mind,
be careful who
you listen to,
what you see,
and what you fill
your mind with.

@joygrantofficial
#frommymesstohismasterpiece

will gather around them a great number of teachers to say what their itching ears want to hear. They will turn their ears away from the truth and turn aside to myths" (NIV). Just because someone agrees with you and affirms you doesn't mean that it is right. Ask yourself this, does what they are saying, or what I am about to do line up with the word of God? If it doesn't then the chances are it is coming from a place of temptation, flesh, opinions, human experiences, and not necessarily from a place of God.

Whatever you are struggling with, God has the answers to keep you walking in your new life and to keep you strong. God wants you to grow and become all that He created you to be.

FEEDING ON THE WORD

Revelation 22:1 says that there is a river of life flowing from the throne of God. We have access to this river through the power of prayer and the reading of God's word. God's word is alive, active, and available to us. Hebrews 4:12 says, "For the word of God is alive and active. Sharper than any double-edged sword, it penetrates even to dividing soul and spirit, joints and marrow; it judges the thoughts and attitudes of the heart" (NIV). Reading the word of God is life to our spirit and bread to our soul. It is the spiritual food that we need to grow.

Jesus is the bread of life. When we go to Him and seek help, He gives us what we need to sustain. John 6:32-35, "Then Jesus said to them, 'Most assuredly, I say to you, Moses did not give you the bread from heaven, but My Father gives you the true bread from heaven. For the bread of God is He who comes down from heaven and gives life to the world. Then they said to Him, 'Lord, give us this bread always.' And Jesus said to them, 'I am the bread of life. He who comes to Me shall never hunger, and he who believes in Me shall never thirst'" (NKJV).

God's word establishes us and gives us direction in the way we should go, especially when we are making decisions that affect our lives. Proverbs 4:20-27 tells us to give attention to His word for these things: "My son, give attention to my words; Incline your ear to my sayings. Do not let them depart from your eyes; Keep them in the midst of your heart; For they are life to those who find them, and health to all their flesh. Keep your heart with all diligence, for out of it spring the issues of life. Put away from you a deceitful mouth and put perverse lips far from you. Let your eyes look straight ahead, and your eyelids look right before you. Ponder the path of your feet and let all your ways be established. Do not turn to the right or the left. Remove your foot from evil" (NKJV).

PRAYER

Through the reading of God's word and through prayer we not only gain direction and perspective for our lives, but we also begin to understand our true purpose. Prayer is a relationship with God. You don't have to stay on your knees all day or repeat certain prayers. It isn't complicated, it is a relationship. It is about praying, but it is also about just talking to Him throughout the day. Staying in a prayerful state of mind gives you the strength you need to resist making the wrong decisions and gives you wisdom from God.

1 Thessalonians 5:17-18 says, "Rejoice always, pray continually, give thanks in all circumstances; for this is God's will for you in Christ Jesus" (NIV). Praying continually is praising Him for the good things around you, it is asking His advice and guidance in the little and the big things.

Every day I ask God to direct my day, to put my hands to work for His glory and according to His will that is written for me in Heaven. God has a specific plan for each one of us, a blueprint for our lives. That is not to control us, but to give us direction and to let us know He has a purpose for us. It allows us to see His plan to bless us as He desires good things for His children. If you have children, you know the joy of seeing them happy on Christmas morning. If you don't have children, perhaps you remember being a child yourself and the feeling of joy receiving the gifts. Matthew 7:9-11 tells us that God wants to see his children blessed even more than we want to see our own children blessed, "Which of you, if your son asks for bread, will give him a stone? Or if he asks for a fish, will give him a snake? If you, then, though you are evil, know how to give good gifts to your children, how much more will your Father in heaven give good gifts to those who ask him!" (NIV).

TEST EVERYTHING BY GOD'S SPIRIT AND BY HIS WORD

Sometimes it is hard to see ourselves like God sees us. We struggle daily with our thoughts and our human emotions, but God sees the good in us. He puts His word in us. His Holy Spirit and His word encourage us to do the right thing, to think the right thoughts, and changes our feelings and emotions towards ourselves and towards others. Jesus doesn't want us to go around feeling inadequate, undeserving or self-hating. He sees us as more than adequate, He sees our full potential, He sees us performing what we were created to do even before we do it. His will is written down for each one of us in Heaven, we only need to ask that it will come to earth to be performed through us. We can find that will through prayer and reading His word. What is His will for your life? It is specific, tailor made just for you, just as mine is tailor made for me. It is what you think about every day, it is a desire locked deep down in your heart, it is a passion put in your heart by God Himself. You only need to seek and ask Him to find it. He will begin to reveal it and guide you to accomplish it.

Test everything by God's spirit and by His word, as it says in 1 John 4:1, "Dear friends, do not believe every spirit, but test the spirits to see whether they are from God, because many false prophets have gone out into the world" (NIV). Drink from His word, the river of life and seek His perfect will for your life. I promise you; you will find it and the strength that you need to overcome every temptation that pulls you away from God.

Chapter 9
STUDY GUIDE

REFLECT Have you ever felt unworthy of God's love?

If you have felt unworthy, what can you do to allow God to "lavish" you with His love?

Are there people in your life who give you advice that is not "sound doctrine" from God?

Can you make a commitment to go to God and His word for answers instead?

Do you know Jesus as your personal savior? Have you prayed to accept Him into your heart?

READ Corinthians 2:9 "Eye has not seen, nor ear heard, nor have entered into the heart of man, the things God has prepared for those who love Him."

1 John 3:1 "See what great love the Father has lavished on us, that we should be called children of God! And that is what we are!"

2 Timothy 4:3-4 "For the time will come when people will not put up with sound doctrine. Instead, to suit their own desires, they will gather around them a great number of teachers to say what their itching ears want to hear. They will turn their ears away from the truth and turn aside to myths."

Hebrews 4:12 "For the word of God is alive and active. Sharper than any double-edged sword, it penetrates even to dividing soul and spirit, joints and marrow; it judges the thoughts and attitudes of the heart."

John 3:16 "For God so loved the world that he gave his one and only Son, that whoever believes in him shall not perish but have eternal life."

2 Corinthians 12:9 "My grace is sufficient for you, for my power is made perfect in weakness. Therefore I will boast all the more gladly of my weaknesses, so that the power of Christ may rest upon me."

DECLARE I am a new creation in Christ! My past is over, Jesus sees it no more! I am set free, delivered and worthy of God's love! I will seek God and His word to grow in my relationship with Him. I make a commitment to Jesus to look forward to my future!

PRAY Father, help me to see and to understand the sacrifice that Jesus made for me on the cross. I want to understand the love that Jesus has for me, and that He died for me so I can live. Thank you for His finished work on the cross, and I invite you, Jesus, into my heart to dwell. Cleanse me and make me whole. Thank you that I AM worthy of your love! I commit my life to you. I thank you that I am truly a new creation in Christ! In Jesus' name I pray. Amen!

Chapter 10
MESSES INTO MASTERPIECES

"For we are God's masterpiece.
He has created us anew in Christ Jesus,
so we can do the good things he planned for us long ago."
Ephesians 2:10 (NLT)

When I began writing this book it was a scattered and unorganized mess; not only on paper, but in my mind. I was frustrated and did not see how it could possibly come together. I had a car accident in 2004 in which I suffered a traumatic brain injury and lost my job. Prior to the accident, writing and organization came easily to me, but afterwards it was very difficult. It affected the left side of my brain, which is the organizational side of the brain. Thankfully, my creative side was not affected, but the prospect of putting a book together seemed monumental and next to impossible.

A good friend and pastor prayed with me about this and said, "It may be scattered now, but God is going to bring it all together." Not only did God help me to slowly put it all together, but He also told me that He was going to turn what I saw as a mess into a masterpiece. Hearing this from God kept me from giving up and saying that I couldn't do it. I'm not suggesting that this book is a masterpiece by the world's standards. It may not make the best-sellers' list; but God has fulfilled His promise in helping me.

MESSES INTO MASTERPIECES

Just as God has helped me with this book, He is in the business of putting our lives back together. He turns our lives and scattered messes into masterpieces. I can relate to this not only from writing, but from the perspective of art. I am an artist and I love to paint. When you begin a painting, you have tubes of paint that are squeezed onto a palette. You mix the colors with a brush, and it doesn't look like anything. It looks like a mess. You would never know that in those tubes of paint lies a painting of maybe the ocean, a portrait of a loved one, or something beautiful. Beginning with a blank canvas, you create. You cannot fathom the beginning to the end, but when you finish you have a beautiful creation.

When we think of artistic masterpieces, we think of the greats: Da Vinci, Michelangelo, Picasso, Rembrandt. Even now when I think of my paintings, I have feelings of inadequacy. Can I *really* create something that is considered a masterpiece? I know by the world's standards I may not create something that can stand up to one of the great artists of our time, but according to God's standards, I can. We have to stop comparing ourselves to what everyone else is doing and look at what God created *each one of us* to do. You *are God's Masterpiece.* He is proud of you. He looks at you and stands back like a great artist and says, "look what I did. I created a masterpiece." He created you out of the palm of His hand. Imagine the time and thought God took into creating you. He chose the color of your eyes, your hair, and your skin. He carefully chose the gifts and talents that you would have. Just as it says in Jeremiah, He ordained you *before* you were even formed in your mother's womb.

You might be thinking now, "He chose the wrong parents for me, I didn't have a good start." Just because you had a bad beginning doesn't mean you have to have a bad ending. Job 8:7 says, "Though your beginning was small, yet your latter end would increase abundantly" (NKJV). Don't be your own worst critic and criticize the work that God has already done in you; there are enough critics in the world for that. There are going to be people who will never see you as good enough. Just as there are art critics who see the flaws in a painting, there will be critics who will only see your flaws; but God sees you as His beautiful masterpiece.

You may see
yourself as a
scattered mess,
but God sees
the beginning
to the end.
He sees a
masterpiece.

You may see yourself as a scattered mess, but God sees the beginning to the end. Ecclesiastes 3:11 says, "He has made everything beautiful in its time. He has also set eternity in the human heart; yet no one can fathom what God has done from beginning to end" (NIV). You are God's canvas and He sees the finished painting before He begins. God made you beautiful, with eternity in mind. He created you unique, with gifts and talents. No one has to offer what you have to offer. No one can reach or touch the people that you can reach. The strokes of the brush on a canvas are like the ups and the downs of your life. In the beginning of a painting, you cannot really tell what it is going to be and sometimes mistakes are made. An art teacher once told me that there are no mistakes in art, you just take what you *think* is a mistake and turn it into something else. I have never forgotten that and have used it not only in art, but as a reminder in life. Just the same, God makes no mistakes. God will take our mistakes and turn them into something else, something beautiful. He will take what was meant to harm you and use it for good.

JOSEPH AND HIS JEALOUS BROTHERS

This is what happened in the book of Genesis with Joseph and the coat of many colors. In this story what was meant for Joseph's harm, was used for good. Joseph's brothers were jealous because their father loved him very much as he was born to him in his old age. Their father presented Joseph with a coat of many colors. God also gave Joseph dreams of the future, signaling that he was destined for royalty. God gave these dreams to Joseph as both encouragement and a warning of things to come. Full of jealousy, his brothers threw him into a pit and sold him into slavery when he was only seventeen years old. Imagine being loved by your father but hated by your brothers so much that they wanted to get rid of you, or even kill you.

Eventually during Joseph's captivity, he was made servant to Potiphar, who was an officer of the Pharaoh of Egypt. Potiphar's wife noticed how young and handsome Joseph was and tried to seduce him. Joseph, being a man of God, rejected her and ran away. She became so angry at his rejection that she falsely accused him of attempting to rape

You will
walk away
from the mess,
turn around
and see
the masterpiece
God has
intended
for you.

her. For this he was thrown into prison. What did he do to deserve all of this? Nothing, nothing, at all. But even though Joseph's life seemed to be a complete mess, he did not become angry or bitter against God or his brothers. Instead, while he was in prison he continued to hear from God; and not only did God continue to give him dreams, but he was also able to interpret dreams.

JOSEPH'S RESPONSE

God also gave Joseph favor with the prison keeper. For two years Joseph stayed in prison, and while there, Pharaoh had a dream that no one could interpret except for Joseph. The Pharaoh's dream was a warning of famine coming to the land of Egypt and Joseph revealed this to Pharaoh. Pharaoh, being so impressed with Joseph and the interpretation of his dream, set Joseph in command over all the land to watch over the crops of Egypt. And when the famine came, because of the wisdom God had given to Joseph, there was plenty of grain in the storehouse for all of Egypt.

The famine was in all the land and when Joseph's father heard that there was food in Egypt, he sent Joseph's brothers to Egypt for food, not knowing Joseph was made governor over the grain. When they arrived, they did not recognize Joseph, but he recognized them. Now, what would you do if you had the power to feed the ones who hurt you and sold you into slavery? Joseph had the power to send them away hungry, or maybe have them killed and get his revenge, but he didn't. Through a series of events Joseph finally reveals himself to his brothers, and they were afraid.

Genesis 45:4, "'Please, come closer,'" he said to them. So, they came closer. And he said again, 'I am Joseph, your brother, whom you sold into slavery in Egypt. But don't be upset, and don't be angry with yourselves for selling me to this place. It was God who sent me here ahead of you to preserve your lives'" (NLT).

"SO NOW IT WAS NOT YOU WHO SENT ME HERE, BUT GOD..."

Joseph realizes that although his brothers betrayed him and sold him into slavery, God turned the situation around to be used for good. Notice he tells his brothers, "So now it was not you who sent me here, but God..." Joseph realizes that what they meant for his harm, God has taken and used for good. Genesis 50:19- 21, "But Joseph said to them, 'Do not be afraid. Am I in the place of God? You intended to harm me, but God intended it for good to accomplish what is now being done, the saving of many lives. So then, do not be afraid.

I will provide for you and your children.' And he reassured them and spoke kindly to them" (NIV).

If you go back and read these chapters for yourself, you will see that Joseph was grieved at the memories of what his brothers had done to him; but in the end, he looked to God, and God showed him the good that was to come. That he was sent to Egypt having endured, and now was going to be a blessing to his family to save them from famine. When Joseph said to his brothers, "Am I in the place of God?" he was saying, I am not your judge, God is. Just as we are not the judge of those who have harmed us, God is. Joseph could have thought his life was a mess and hopeless, but God turned it around and made it into a masterpiece.

HE WILL MAKE THE END ABUNDANT
Joseph was as close to the personification of Jesus as any human being has ever been. He was loved by his father and betrayed by his brothers, yet he forgave them; not only did he forgive them, but he blessed them. Did Joseph's brothers deserve to be blessed? In our eyes, no; but in God's eyes, yes. Joseph put aside his judgement and emotions and gave God the ultimate glory by blessing his family with more than they deserved. As such, God desires to do so with our lives.

Psalms 115:14-15 says, "The Lord shall increase you more and more, you and your children" (KJV). God wants to bless you more and more, even though your beginning seems small and messed up, He will make the end abundant. As Joseph said to his brothers, God is saying to you, the blessing will flow from you to your children and your children's children. There is no end to what God can do. What was meant for your harm, as Joseph said, will be turned by God and used for your good. You will walk away from the mess, turn around and see the masterpiece God has intended for you.

Joseph was thirty years old when he became Governor over the crops of Egypt. So, for thirteen years, from the time his brothers put him into the pit at seventeen until he stood before Pharaoh, his life seemed like a mess. But because Joseph continued to seek God during those thirteen years; God continued to use him, even in prison. What appeared to be his doom brought him to victory. He was delivered from the depths of his chains and set free. Suddenly, God delivered Joseph to a place of royalty, just like the dreams he had as a young man, God was beginning to fulfill them. I'm sure that Joseph never forgot those dreams as he sat in a damp, dirty prison cell; and I'm sure those dreams kept Joseph's hopes alive. Joseph went from the pit to royalty.

HE CAN CHANGE YOUR LIFE

The same way that God blessed Joseph, He desires to bless you. You may look around you and say, I'm still in the middle of the mess. I'm an addict, I'm depressed, I'm not feeling well, I'm broke, look at me I'm no good; but that isn't God, that's the enemy lying to you. God has a voice, and the enemy has a voice. They are both real, and God is saying to you, you are beautiful, you are lovely, you are my chosen one; I have a plan for you, I have a good inheritance for you. Psalms 16:5-6 says, "O Lord, You are the portion of my inheritance and my cup; You maintain my lot. The lines have fallen to me in pleasant places; Yes, I have a good inheritance" (NKJV). Sometimes you have to put aside your feelings and make a decision to believe God.

Jeremiah 29:11 says, "'For I know the plans I have for you,' declares the Lord, 'plans to prosper you and not to harm you, plans to give you hope and a future. Then you will call on me and come and pray to me, and I will listen to you. You will seek me and find me when you seek me with all your heart. I will be found by you,' declares the Lord, 'and will bring you back from captivity. I will gather you from all the nations and places where I have banished you,' declares the Lord, 'and will bring you back to the place from which I carried you into exile'" (NIV). You may feel like you are in "exile;" far, far away from God; and I'm sure Joseph felt banished and in exile when he was sold into slavery. But as His word says if you seek God, you *will* find Him, and He will bring you back. In a moment, in the twinkling of an eye, He can change your life and turn it around.

In the Book of John, the disciples were afraid, lost at sea in the middle of a storm. Jesus appeared to them walking on the water, and when Jesus got onto the boat with them, they were *immediately* delivered to the shore. John 6:18-21, "A strong wind was blowing and the waters grew rough. When they had rowed about three or four miles, they saw Jesus approaching the boat, walking on the water; and they were frightened. But he said to them, 'It is I; do not be afraid.' Then they were willing to take him into the boat, *and immediately* the boat reached the shore where they were heading" (NIV).

They were at sea, lost, afraid and in a storm, then Jesus showed up and they were immediately saved. Jesus doesn't waste time when you receive Him into your life, He immediately delivers you. He immediately begins to turn your life around, and your sorrow into joy. Psalms 30:11-12, "You have turned my mourning into dancing for me; You have taken off my sackcloth and clothed me with joy..." (AMP).

Jesus wants to take *your* mess and turn it into a masterpiece, just as He has taken mine. Don't wait for everything to be perfect before you allow Him to change your life; life will never be perfect. There will never be a more perfect time than now. You *are* good enough now, you *are* perfect enough now, you *are* worthy enough now and He loves you. Remember who you are, you are a child of the Most-High God! You *are* God's Masterpiece!

HOW DO I BEGIN THIS JOURNEY?

"For God so loved the world that he gave his one and only Son,
that whoever believes in him shall not perish but have eternal life.
For God did not send his Son into the world to condemn the world,
but to save the world through him."
John 3:16-17 (NIV)

Thank you for reading this far and taking this journey with me. I hope by the time you have reached this point of the book that you have forgotten what the beginning was about. In other words, I hope that you only remember the good things about Jesus and how He can change your life. As it says in Philippians 4:8, think on the good things: "Finally, brethren, whatsoever things are true, whatsoever things are honest, whatsoever things are just, whatsoever things are pure, whatsoever things are lovely, whatsoever things are of good report; if there be any virtue, and if there be any praise, think on these things" (KJV).

Just as I have forgotten my past and am a new creation in Christ, when you begin living your new life in Christ, you will start to forget your past, too. Of course, we don't have the gift of actually forgetting as God does; but through God's ability to heal, we are supernaturally made new. God says in Psalms 103:12 our sins are cast "as far as the east is from the west, so far has he removed our transgressions from us" (NIV). And Hebrews 8:12 tells us He remembers them no more, "For I will be merciful to their unrighteousness, and their sins and their iniquities will I remember no more" (KJV). God has the ability to forget our past, He doesn't spend any time thinking about it, and neither should you.

THE MOST IMPORTANT PRAYER YOU WILL EVER PRAY

You might be thinking, "This is all great, but I don't even know where to begin." It begins with the basics; a relationship with Jesus Christ by asking Him into your heart. So, if by now you have not asked Jesus into your life, now is the time. This is the place to pause and pray. John 10:27-30 says, "My sheep hear my voice, and I know them, and they follow me.

I give them eternal life, and they will never perish, and no one will snatch them out of my hand. My Father, who has given them to me, is greater than all, and no one is able to snatch them out of the Father's hand. I and the Father are one" (ESV). After you pray this prayer, you can never be snatched out of the Father's hand. He will hold firmly to you, be your protector and your guide as you continue to seek and follow Him all the days of your life. Just pray this simple prayer and you will be forever written into the Lamb's Book of Life:

"Lord Jesus, I believe that you died for me on the cross and rose again. Please forgive me of my sins and come into my heart. I want to make you my Lord and my Savior. Help me to follow you and serve you all the days of my life. I thank you, Jesus, that my name is now written in The Lamb's Book of Life, and no one can snatch me out of the palm of your hand. In Jesus' Name I pray, Amen." Now it's time to celebrate, a new life has been given to you! Your name has been written in the Lamb's Book of Life in Heaven and no one can take that away from you. It is for all of eternity!

It is extremely important now to get the support you need by finding a good Bible-based church in your area. Surround yourself with people who are like minded, who will love you, and who will pray for you. We were never meant to walk alone, even Jesus surrounded himself with his friends and disciples. We all need love and support; it is how we were created to be. Remember, God has a place for you!

TELL YOUR STORY - DON'T BE ASHAMED OF YOUR SCARS

"Go into all the world and preach the gospel to all creation."
Mark 16:15 (NIV)

Now that you know you are born again into the kingdom of God, you have a story to tell, a testimony to give. Your testimony lies in your scars, the things you have been through that will help others. Jesus has scars. When Jesus arose from the tomb, He could have come back to life complete in his body with no scars, but he chose to keep the scars in His hands, His feet, and His side. Not because he needed to prove anything to anyone, but because he was proud of his scars. Even Jesus had a testimony to give of what He suffered through and overcame. His scars were His proof.

JESUS WEARS HIS SCARS

Jesus' life was not easy. He was born during a time of Roman tyranny and Satan tried to destroy His life from the beginning. His mother Mary was almost stoned to death for being pregnant and unwed, and after His birth, King Herod tried to murder Him by ordering all babies two and under to be killed. I believe the soldiers did not take the time to see the sex of the babies but killed indiscriminately looking for Jesus. What a terrible time in history. Mary and Joseph escaped with Jesus only because of the warning from an angel who appeared to Joseph. What if Joseph didn't listen to that angel? What if he thought it was just a dream and stayed?

Life for our Savior was not any easier when He began his ministry. He was the son of a carpenter and rejected as a prophet by his hometown of Nazareth. Mark 6:3-6, "'Isn't this the carpenter? Isn't this Mary's son and the brother of James, Joseph, Judas, and Simon? Aren't his sisters here with us?' And they took offense at him. Jesus said to them, 'A prophet is not without honor except in his own town, among his relatives and in his own home.' He could not do any miracles there, except lay his hands on a few sick people and heal them. He was amazed at their lack of faith" (NIV). And in Jesus' own words, Luke 4:24, "'Truly I tell you,' He continued, 'no prophet is accepted in his hometown'" (NIV).

Jesus was despised by the Pharisees (the "judgmental and religious" folk), rejected by those he healed, denied by those closest to him and crucified by those he loved. After He arose from the dead, He showed himself to the disciples in the upper room and Thomas doubted that it was Him. Jesus seeing this showed Thomas His battle scars. Those scars were proof to Thomas that it indeed was Him and that He truly arose from the dead. Jesus wears his scars as a story of what He went through for us and so should we.

SHARED SCARS MAKE US STRONGER
Revelation 12:10-11 says that we overcome by the blood of the Lamb and the word of our testimony, "Then I heard a loud voice saying in heaven, "Now salvation, and strength, and the kingdom of our God, and the power of His Christ have come, for the accuser of our brethren, who accused them before our God day and night, has been cast down. And they overcame him by the blood of the Lamb and by the word of their testimony, and they did not love their lives to the death" (NKJV). Who do we overcome? The enemy. The more we share our testimony and show our scars, the stronger we become. Why do you think the enemy wants to keep you quiet and ashamed? Because many like you are waiting to be healed.

Recently, I went to the dentist, and they told me I had a "strong tongue." It wouldn't stay out of their way to do the dental work. I found it funny, but then I realized, "Hey, I do have a strong tongue." I'm not the shy little girl my father said I was; God has given me a voice to use with my tongue, and the ability to share my story and testimony. The same stands for you. When we are redeemed by Jesus, we can point to our scars and say, "Look what Jesus has done for me!"

Our scars are from the mistakes of our past. Jesus had scars that were not *from His sin*, but *for our sins*. He allowed Himself to be bruised, beaten and crucified for *us*. When Jesus said on the cross "it is finished" it was because He had finished the redemptive work of His Father. He had shed His blood for *our sins*. He could have said, "Now Father remove these scars from my hands, my feet, and my side. I don't want to be reminded of what I went through on earth," but He didn't. He kept His scars as a sign and proof of who He is and what He has done for us. He is proud of His scars because of His living testimony of who He is. Jesus wants the same for us.

WE ALL HAVE A DESTINY
Lay down the shame of your past. When it tries to creep up and say, "you can't tell people what you've done. You'll be embarrassed, you were such a bad person;" remember those are lies from the enemy trying to keep

you quiet. The enemy doesn't want you to talk about your battle scars. He wants you to hide them, keep them secret, and move on. But God wants you to show them, talk about them, and be proud of them because His Son took those scars for you on the cross. They are no longer wounds, festering and causing infection in your life, they are scars; healed, whole, and clean because of the blood of Jesus.

Your scars are different than my scars. Your scars can reach people that I can't; just as my scars can reach people that your scars can't. In that sense we all have a destiny; a crowd of people God has assigned to us to reach. Roll up your sleeves and show those scars to the ones who are still in the same battle that you've been rescued from. Telling our stories is not only important for others, but to remind ourselves of where we came from and what He delivered us from. That is not to remember in guilt or shame, but to rejoice that it was not by our doing for it was by His grace that we were saved.

GO INTO ALL THE WORLD

In Mark 16:15, one of Jesus' last instructions while on earth, before He ascended into Heaven was to, "Go into all the world and preach the gospel to every creature." How do you preach the gospel to every creature? By telling your story about what He has done for you. Most of all persevere and as it says in 2 Chronicles 15:7, "But as for you, be strong and do not give up, for your work will be rewarded" (NIV). So, persevere, be proud and excited! Tell everyone what Jesus has done for you!

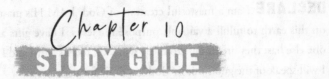

Chapter 10

STUDY GUIDE

REFLECT Despite the ups and downs of life, you are a constant work of art in God's hands. Can you see yourself as God's beautiful creation?

Do you believe that God created you with a divine purpose to fulfill here on the earth?

What do you believe that purpose is? If you are not sure, will you seek Him for an answer?

You have a valuable story to tell! Will you look to God and begin to share it?

READ Ephesians 2:10 "For we are God's masterpiece. He has created us anew in Christ Jesus, so we can do the good things he planned for us long ago."

Ecclesiastes 3:11 "He has made everything beautiful in its time. He has also set eternity in the human heart; yet no one can fathom what God has done from beginning to end."

Job 8:7 "Though your beginning was small, yet your latter end would increase abundantly."

2 Timothy 1:7 "For God has not given us a spirit of fear, but of power and of love and of a sound mind."

Mark 16:15 "Go into all the world and preach the gospel to all creation."

DECLARE I am a masterful creation of God. I AM His masterpiece! I was put on this earth to fulfill a valuable purpose for Jesus. I have gifts and talents that no one else has; they are unique to me. I will look to His word and I will not be afraid! I will speak of the good things God has done for me!

PRAY Lord, thank you for seeing me as your vessel; worthy to speak your Name. I ask you for the courage and strength that I need to be a witness for you. I will tell of your love, your mercy and your kindness. I want to fulfill all your purposes for me here on earth as it is written in Heaven. I thank you for directing me in your perfect path! I make a commitment to serve you all the days of my life. In Jesus' name I pray. Amen!

Scriptures

"Finally, brethren, whatsoever things are true, whatsoever things are honest, whatsoever things are just, whatsoever things are pure, whatsoever things are lovely, whatsoever things are of good report; if there be any virtue, and if there be any praise, think on these things."

Philippians 4:8 (KJV)

On the following pages I have created a guide to the scriptures referenced in this book. No word spoken by me is more important than the Word of God. My words tell my story, but God's word will change your life.

As you begin your journey with Jesus you will have joyful, fruitful seasons; but you will also have dry, desert seasons. Use His word referenced here and, more importantly, in your Bible as it says in Psalms 119:105, as a lamp unto your feet and a light unto your path.

Know that He is always with you and will never forsake you. He will rejoice with you in the good times, will walk beside you in the bad times, and He will always bring you out of the desert.

CHAPTER 1

Romans 7:15, "I do not understand what I do. For what I want to do I do not do, but what I hate I do." (NIV)

1 Peter 4:8, "Above all, love each other deeply, because love covers over a multitude of sins." (NIV)

Deuteronomy 30:2-4, "(when) you have returned to the Lord your God and have listened to and obeyed His voice with all your heart and with all your soul, in accordance with everything that I am commanding you today, you and your children, then the Lord your God will restore your fortunes, and have compassion on you, and will gather you together again from all the peoples where He has scattered you. Even if any of your dispersed are at the ends of the earth, the Lord your God will gather you together from there, and from there He will bring you back." (AMP)

Psalms 25:5, "Guide me in your truth and teach me, for you are God my Savior, and my hope is in you all day long." (NIV)

Romans 12:2, "Do not conform to the pattern of this world, but be transformed by the renewing of your mind. Then you will be able to test and approve what God's will is--his good, pleasing and perfect will." (NIV)

Romans 8:5-6, "Those who live according to the flesh have their minds set on what the flesh desires; but those who live in accordance with the Spirit have their minds set on what the Spirit desires. The mind governed by the flesh is death, but the mind governed by the Spirit is life and peace." (NIV)

Romans 3:23, "All have sinned and fall short of the glory of God." (NIV)

Matthew 7:1-2, "Do not judge, or you too will be judged. For in the same way you judge others, you will be judged, and with the measure you use, it will be measured to you." (NIV)

Ephesians 3:16-18, "I pray that out of His glorious riches He may strengthen you with power through His Spirit in your inner being, so that Christ may dwell in your hearts *through faith. And I pray that you, being rooted and established in love, may have power, together with all the Lord's holy people, to grasp how wide and long and high and deep is the love of Christ, and to know this love that surpasses knowledge - that you may be filled to measure of all the fullness of God." (NIV)*

CHAPTER 2

1 John 3:1, "See what great love the Father has lavished on us, that we should be called children of God!" (NIV)

Proverbs 18:21, "Death and life are in the power of the tongue, and those who love it will eat its fruit. (NKJV)

1 Corinthians 6:18, "Flee sexual immorality. Every sin that a man does is outside the body, but he who commits sexual immorality sins against his own body." (KJV)

1 Peter 5:8, "Be sober, be vigilant; because your adversary the devil walks about like a roaring lion, seeking whom he may devour." (NKJV)

2Chronicles 16:9, "For the eyes of the Lord move to and fro throughout the earth so that He may support those whose heart is completely His. You have acted foolishly in this; therefore, from now on you will have wars." (AMP)

Psalms 34:17, "When the righteous cry for help, the Lord hears and delivers them out of all their troubles." (ESV)

1 Corinthians 6:19-20, "Do you not know that your bodies are temples of the Holy Spirit, who is in you, whom you have received from God? You are not your own; you were bought at a price. Therefore honor God with your bodies." (NIV)

John 2:13-16, "When it was almost time for the Jewish Passover, Jesus went up to Jerusalem. In the temple courts he found people selling cattle, sheep and doves, and others sitting at tables exchanging money. So, he made a whip out of cords, and drove all from the temple courts, both sheep and cattle; he scattered the coins of the money changers and overturned their tables. To those who sold doves he said, 'Get these out of here! Stop turning my Father's house into a market!'" (NIV)

CHAPTER 3

1 Peter 2:9, "But you are a chosen people, a royal priesthood, a holy nation, God's special possession, that you may declare the praises of him who called you out of darkness into his wonderful light." (NIV)

2 Corinthians 11:14, "Even Satan disguises himself as an angel of light." (NLT)

Matthew 4:8-10, "Again, the devil took him to a very high mountain and showed him all the kingdoms of the world and their splendor. 'All this I will give you,' he said, 'if you will bow down and worship me.' Jesus said to him, 'Away from me, Satan! For it is written: 'Worship the Lord your God, and serve him only.'" (NIV)

Genesis 50:20, "You intended to harm me, but God intended it for good to accomplish what is now being done, the saving of many lives." (NIV)

Job 8:5-7, "But if you will seek God earnestly and plead with the Almighty, if you are pure and upright, even now He will rouse Himself on your behalf and restore you to your prosperous state. Your beginnings will seem humble, so prosperous will your future be." (NIV)

Psalms 139:13, "For you created my inmost being; you knit me together in my mother's womb." (AMP)

Isaiah 5:20-21, "Woe to those who call evil good and good evil, who put darkness for light and light for darkness, who put bitter for sweet and sweet for bitter. Woe to those who are wise in their own eyes and clever in their own sight." (NIV)

Hebrews 3:7, "So, as the Holy Spirit says: "Today, if you hear his voice, do not harden your hearts." (NIV)

Jeremiah 1:5, "Before I formed you in the womb I knew you, before you were born I set you apart; I appointed you as a prophet to the nations." (NIV)

Psalms 139:13-16, "For you created my inmost being; you knit me together in my mother's womb. I praise you because I am fearfully and wonderfully made; your works are wonderful, I know that full well. My frame was not hidden from you when I was made in the secret place, when I was woven together in the depths of the earth. Your eyes saw my unformed body; all the days ordained for me were written in your book before one of them came to be." (NIV)

Acts 28:27, "For this people's heart has become calloused; they hardly hear with their ears, and they have closed their eyes. Otherwise they might see with their eyes, hear with their ears, understand with their hearts and turn, and I would heal them." (NIV)

Psalms 103:2-5, "Praise the Lord, my soul, and forget not all his benefits-who forgives all your sins and heals all your diseases, who redeems your life from the pit and crowns you with love and compassion, who satisfies your desires with good things so that your youth is renewed like the eagle's." (NIV)

John 8:1-11, "Jesus returned to the Mount of Olives, but early the next morning he was back again at the Temple. A crowd soon gathered, and he sat down and taught them. As he was speaking, the teachers of religious law and the Pharisees brought a woman who had been caught in the act of adultery. They put her in front of the crowd. 'Teacher,' they said to Jesus, 'this woman was caught in the act of adultery. The law of Moses says to stone her. What do you say?' They were trying to trap Him into saying something they could use against him, but Jesus stooped down and wrote in the dust with his finger. They kept demanding an answer, so He stood up again and said, 'All right, but let the one who has never sinned throw the first stone!' Then He stooped down again and wrote in the dust. When the accusers heard this, they slipped away one by one, beginning with the oldest, until only Jesus was left in the middle of the crowd with the woman. Then Jesus stood up again and said to the woman, 'Where are your accusers? Didn't even one of them condemn you?' 'No, Lord,' she said. And Jesus said, 'Neither do I. Go and sin no more.'" (NLT)

Isaiah 1:18, "Come now, and let us reason together," saith the Lord. "Though your sins be as scarlet, they shall be as white as snow; though they be red like crimson, they shall be as wool." (KJV)

CHAPTER 4

John 5:30, "By myself I can do nothing..." (NIV)

Deuteronomy 30:19, "This day I call the heavens and the earth as witnesses against you that I have set before you life and death, blessings and curses. Now choose life, so that you and your children may live." (NIV)

John 6:63, "It is the Spirit who gives life; the flesh is no help at all. The words that I have spoken to you are spirit and life." (ESV)

Matthew 8:5-13, "When Jesus had entered Capernaum, a centurion came to Him asking for help. 'Lord,' he said, 'my servant lies at home paralyzed, suffering terribly.' Jesus said to him, 'Shall I come and heal him. The centurion replied, 'Lord, I do not deserve to have you come under my roof. But just say the word, and my servant will be healed. For I myself am a man under authority, with soldiers under me. I tell this one, 'Go,' and he goes; and that one, 'Come,' and he comes. I say to my servant, 'Do this,' and he does it,' and will. When Jesus heard this, he was amazed and said to those following him, 'Truly I tell you, I have not found anyone in Israel with such great faith...' Then Jesus said to the centurion, 'Go! Let it be done just as you believed it would.' And his servant was healed at that moment." (NIV)

Isaiah 40:31, "But they that wait upon the LORD shall renew their strength" (KJV)

Isaiah 40:30, "Even youths grow tired and weary, and young men stumble and fall..." (NIV)

John 8:44, "He was a murderer from the beginning, and does not stand in the truth, because there is no truth in him. When he lies, he speaks out of his own character, for he is a liar and the father of lies." (ESV)

Zechariah 3:1, "Then the angel showed me Joshua the high priest standing before the Angel of the LORD, with Satan standing at his right hand to accuse him." (NIV)

Genesis 16:1-6, "Now Sarai, Abram's wife, had not been able to bear children for him. But she had an Egyptian servant named Hagar. So, Sarai said to Abram, 'The LORD has prevented me from having children.'" (Notice she is blaming God instead of believing His promises.) *"'Go and sleep with my servant. Perhaps I can have children through her.' And Abram agreed with Sarai's proposal. So, Sarai, Abram's wife, took Hagar the Egyptian servant and gave her to Abram as a wife"* (This happened ten years after Abram had settled in the land of Canaan. Ten years after the promise of a child) "So Abram had sexual relations with Hagar, and she became pregnant. But when Hagar knew she was pregnant, she began to treat her mistress, Sarai, with contempt. Then Sarai said to Abram, 'This is all your fault! I put my servant into your arms, but now that she's pregnant she treats me with contempt. The LORD will show who's wrong—you or me!'" (Now she's blaming her husband for their mistake!) "Abram replied, 'Look, she is your servant, so deal with her as you see fit.' Then Sarai treated Hagar so harshly that she finally ran away." (NLT)

Genesis 16:7-10, "The angel of the LORD found Hagar beside a spring of water in the wilderness, along the road to Shur. The angel said to her, 'Hagar, Sarai's servant, where have you come from, and where are you going?' 'I'm running away from my mistress, Sarai,' she replied. The angel of the LORD said to her, 'Return to your mistress, and submit to her authority.' Then he added, 'I will give you more descendants than you can count.'" (NLT)

Genesis 17:17-18, "Then Abraham bowed down to the ground, but he laughed to himself in disbelief. 'How could I become a father at the age of 100?' he thought. 'And how can Sarah have a baby when she is ninety years old?' So, Abraham said to God, 'May Ishmael live under your special blessing!'" (AMP)

Genesis 17:19, "But God said, 'No, Sarah your wife shall bear you a son indeed, and you shall name him Isaac (laughter); and I will establish My covenant with him for an everlasting covenant and with his descendants after him.'" (AMP)

Genesis 18:13-14, "And the Lord said to Abraham, 'Why did Sarah laugh, saying, 'Shall I surely bear a child, since I am old?' Is anything too hard for the Lord? At the appointed time I will return to you, according to the time of life, and Sarah shall have a son.'" (NKJV)

Genesis 21:1-3, "The Lord graciously remembered and visited Sarah as He had said, and the Lord did for her as He had promised. So, Sarah conceived and gave birth to a son for Abraham in his old age, at the appointed time of which God had spoken to him. Abraham named his son Isaac (laughter), the son to whom Sarah gave birth." (AMP)

Genesis 21:9-11, "Now [as time went on] Sarah saw [Ishmael] the son of Hagar the Egyptian, whom she had borne to Abraham, mocking [Isaac]. Therefore, she said to Abraham, 'Drive out this maid and her son, for the son of this maid shall not be an heir with my son Isaac.' The situation distressed Abraham greatly because of his son [Ishmael]." (AMP)

Genesis 16:12, "This son of yours will be a wild man, as untamed as a wild donkey! He will raise his fist against everyone, and everyone will be against him. Yes, he will live in open hostility against all his relatives." (NLT)

Proverbs 3:5-6, "Trust in the Lord with all your heart, and lean not on your own understanding; In all your ways acknowledge Him, and He shall direct your paths." (NKJV)

Habakkuk 2:3, "For the vision is yet for an appointed time, but at the end it shall speak, and not lie: though it tarry, wait for it; because it will surely come, it will not tarry." (NKJV)

Psalms 16:2, "O my soul, you have said to the Lord, You are my Lord, my goodness is nothing apart from You." (NKJV)

Romans 8:5, "Those who live according to the flesh have their minds set on what the flesh desires; but those who live in accordance with the Spirit have their minds set on what the Spirit desires." (NIV)

Romans 8:6, "The mind governed by the flesh is death, but the mind governed by the Spirit is life and peace." (NIV)

Proverbs 23:7, "For as he thinks in his heart, so is he." (NKJV)

Romans 8:7-8, "The mind governed by the flesh is hostile to God; it does not submit to God's law, nor can it do so. Those who are in the realm of the flesh cannot please God." (NIV)

Romans 7:19, "I want to do what is good, but I don't. I don't want to do what is wrong, but I do it anyway." (NLT)

2 Peter 2:21-22, "It would have been better for them not to have known the way of righteousness, than to have known it and then to turn their backs on the sacred command that was passed on to them. Of them the proverbs are true: 'A dog returns to its vomit,' and, 'A sow that is washed returns to her wallowing in the mud.'" (NIV)

Proverbs 26:11, "Like a dog that returns to his vomit is a fool who repeats his foolishness." (NASB)

Psalms 16:1-2, "Preserve me, O God, for in You I put my Trust. O my soul, you have said to the Lord, You are my Lord, my goodness is nothing apart from You." (NKJV)

Isaiah 54:5, "For your husband is your Maker, Whose name is the LORD of hosts; And your Redeemer is the Holy One of Israel, Who is called the God of all the earth." (NKJV)

Isaiah 30:21, "Whether you turn to the right or to the left, your ears will hear a voice behind you, saying, 'This is the way; walk in it.'" (NIV)

Hebrews 10:26-27, "For if we go on sinning willfully after receiving the knowledge of the truth, there no longer remains a sacrifice for sins, but a terrifying expectation of judgement and THE FURY OF A FIRE WHICH CONSUME THE ADVERSARIES." (NASB)

CHAPTER 5

1 Corinthians 10:13, "No temptation has overtaken you except what is common to mankind. And God is faithful; he will not let you be tempted beyond what you can bear. But when you are tempted, he will also provide a way out so that you can endure it." (NIV)

Psalms 34:4-5, "I sought the Lord, and he answered me; he delivered me from all my fears. Those who look to Him are radiant; their faces are never covered with shame." (NIV)

Isaiah 30:21, "Whether you turn to the right or to the left, your ears will hear a voice behind you saying, 'This is the way; walk in it.'" (NIV)

Judges 14:12-14, "Let me tell you a riddle," Samson said to them. "If you can give me the answer within the seven days of the feast, I will give you thirty linen garments and thirty sets of clothes. If you can't tell me the answer, you must give me thirty linen garments and thirty sets of clothes. 'Tell us your riddle,' they said. 'Let's hear it.' He replied, 'Out of the eater, something to eat; out of the strong, something sweet.'" (NIV)

Judges 14:15-16, "On the fourth a day, they said to Samson's wife, 'Coax your husband into explaining the riddle for us, or we will burn you and your father's household to death. Did you invite us here to steal our property?' Then Samson's wife threw herself on him, sobbing, 'You hate me! You don't really love me. You've given my people a riddle, but you haven't told me the answer.' 'I haven't even explained it to my father or mother,' he replied, 'so why should I explain it to you?' She cried the whole seven days of the feast. So, on the seventh day he finally told her, because she continued to press him. She in turn explained the riddle to her people." (NIV)

Judges 16:4-6, "Sometime later, he fell in love with a woman in the Valley of Sorek whose name was Delilah. The rulers of the Philistines went to her and said, 'See if you can lure him into showing you the secret of his great strength and how we can overpower him so we may tie him up and subdue him. Each one of us will give you eleven hundred shekels of silver.' So, Delilah said to Samson, 'Tell me the secret of your great strength and how you can be tied up and subdued.'" (NIV)

Judges 16:15-21, "Then she said to him, 'How can you say, 'I love you,' when you won't confide in me? This is the third time you have made a fool of me and haven't told me the secret of your great strength.' With such nagging she prodded him day after day until he was sick to death of it. So, he told her everything. No razor has ever been used on my head,' he said, 'because I have been a Nazirite dedicated to God from my mother's womb. If my head were shaved, my strength would leave me, and I would become as weak as any other man.' When Delilah saw that he had told her everything, she sent word to the rulers of the Philistines, 'Come back once more; he has told me everything.' So, the rulers of the Philistines returned with the silver in their hands. After putting him to sleep on her lap, she called for someone to shave off the seven braids of his hair, and so began to subdue him. And his strength left him. Then she called, 'Samson, the Philistines are upon you!' He awoke from his sleep and thought, 'I'll go out as before and shake myself free.' But he did not know that the

Lord had left him. Then the Philistines seized him, gouged out his eyes and took him down to Gaza. Binding him with bronze shackles, they set him to grinding grain in the prison." (NIV)

1 Peter 5:8-9, "Be alert and of sober mind. Your enemy the devil prowls around like a roaring lion looking for someone to devour. Resist him, standing firm in the faith, because you know that the family of believers throughout the world is undergoing the same kind of sufferings." (NIV)

Isaiah 61:7, "Instead of your shame you will receive a double portion, and instead of disgrace you will rejoice in your inheritance. And so you will inherit a double portion in your land, and everlasting joy will be yours." (NIV)

Deuteronomy 30:3-14, "God, your God, will restore everything you lost; he'll have compassion on you; he'll come back and pick up the pieces from all the places where you were scattered. No matter how far away you end up, God, your God, will get you out of there and bring you back to the land your ancestors once possessed. It will be yours again. He will give you a good life and make you more numerous than your ancestors. God, your God, will cut away the thick calluses on your heart and your children's hearts, freeing you to love God, your God, with your whole heart and soul and live, really live. God, your God, will put all these curses on your enemies who hated you and were out to get you. And you will make a new start, listening obediently to God, keeping all his commandments that I'm commanding you today. God, your God, will outdo himself in making things go well for you: you will have babies, get calves, grow crops, and enjoy an all-around good life. Yes, God will start enjoying you again, making things go well for you just as he enjoyed doing it for your ancestors. But only if you listen obediently to God, your God, and keep the commandments and regulations written in this Book of Revelation. Nothing halfhearted here; you must return to God, your God, totally, heart and soul, holding nothing back. This commandment that I am commanding you today isn't too much for you, it's not out of your reach. It's not on a high mountain - you do not have to get mountaineers to climb the peak and bring it down to your level and explain it before you can live it. And it's not across the ocean - you do not have to send sailors out to get it, bring it back, and then explain it before you can live it. No. The word is right here and now- as near as the tongue in your mouth, as near as the heart in your chest. Just do it!" (MSG)

Psalms 18:48, "He delivers me from my enemies. You also lift me up above those who rise against me; You have delivered me from the violent man." (NKJV)

Genesis 22:1-2, "Sometime later God tested Abraham. He said to him, 'Abraham!' 'Here I am,' he replied. Then God said, 'Take your son, your only son, whom you love—Isaac—and go to the region of Moriah. Sacrifice him there as a burnt offering on a mountain I will show you.'" (NIV)

Genesis 22:9-12, "When they reached the place God had told him about, Abraham built an altar there and arranged the wood on it. He bound his son Isaac and laid him on the altar, on top of the wood. Then he reached out his hand and took the knife to slay his son. But the angel of the Lord called out to him from heaven, 'Abraham! Abraham!' 'Here I am,' he replied. 'Do not lay a hand on the boy,' he said. 'Do not do anything to him. Now I know that you fear God, because you have not withheld from me your son, your only son.' Abraham looked up and there in a thicket he saw a ram caught by its horns. He went over and took the ram and sacrificed it as a burnt offering instead of his son." (NIV)

Ephesians 5:1, "Follow God's example, therefore, as dearly loved children and walk in the way of love, just as Christ loved us and gave himself up for us as a fragrant offering and sacrifice to God." (NIV)

Ephesians 5:25-30, "Husbands, love your wives, just as Christ loved the church and gave himself up for her to make her holy, cleansing her by the washing with water through the word, and to present her to himself as a radiant church, without stain or wrinkle or any other blemish, but holy and blameless. In this same way, husbands ought to love their wives as their own bodies. He who loves his wife loves himself. After all, no one ever hated their own body, but they feed and care for their body, just as Christ does the church for we are members of his body." (NIV)

John 15:13, "Greater love has no one than this, than to lay down one's life for his friends." (NKJV)

Genesis 1:27, "So God created mankind in his own image, in the image of God he created them; male and female he created them." (KJV)

Psalms 103:8-13, "The LORD is compassionate and merciful, slow to get angry and filled with unfailing love. He will not constantly accuse us, nor remain angry forever. He does not punish us for all our sins; he does not deal harshly with us, as we deserve. For his unfailing love toward those who fear him is as great as the height of the heavens above the earth. He has removed our sins as far from us as the east is from the west. The LORD is like a father to his children, tender and compassionate to those who fear him." *(NLT)*

Proverbs 18:10, "The name of the LORD is a strong tower; The righteous run to it and are safe." *(NKJV)*

Psalms 91:1-2, "Whoever dwells in the shelter of the Most-High will rest in the shadow of the Almighty. I will say of the Lord, 'He is my refuge and my fortress, my God, in whom I trust.'" *(NIV)*

Matthew 7:9-11, "Which of you, if your son asks for bread, will give him a stone? Or if he asks for a fish, will give him a snake? If you, then, though you are evil, know how to give good gifts to your children, how much more will your Father in heaven give good gifts to those who ask him!" *(NIV)*

Psalms 25:12, "Who is the man who fears the Lord? He will instruct him in the way that he should choose." *(ESV)*

Psalms 32:8, "I will instruct you and teach you in the way which you should go; I will counsel you with My eye upon you." *(ESV)*

Isaiah 28:6, "For his God instructs and teaches him properly." *(NASB)*

Isaiah 54:13, "All your children will be taught by the LORD, and great will be their peace." *(NIV)*

Hebrews 12:5, "My son, do not make light of the Lord's discipline, and do not lose heart when he rebukes you, because the Lord disciplines the one he loves, and he chastens everyone he accepts as his son." *(NIV)*

Deuteronomy 8:5, "Know then in your heart that as a man disciplines his son, so the LORD your God disciplines you." (NIV)

Job 5:17, "Behold, happy is the person whom God disciplines, so do not reject the discipline of the Almighty." (NASB)

1 Corinthians 11:32, "Yet when we are judged by the Lord, we are being disciplined so that we will not be condemned along with the world." (NLT)

Isaiah 48:17, "Thus says the Lord, your Redeemer, the Holy One of Israel, 'I am the Lord your God, who teaches you to profit, Who leads you in the way you should go.'" (NKJV)

Deuteronomy 32:9-12, "For the people of Israel belong to the LORD; Jacob is his special possession. He found them in a desert land, in an empty, howling wasteland. He surrounded them and watched over them; he guarded them as he would guard his own eyes. Like an eagle that rouses her chicks and hovers over her young, so he spread his wings to take them up and carried them safely on his pinions. The LORD alone guided them; they followed no foreign gods." (NLT)

2 Peter 3:9, "The Lord is not slow in keeping his promise, as some understand slowness. Instead, he is patient with you, not wanting anyone to perish, but everyone to come to repentance." (NIV)

Jeremiah 17:7-8, "But blessed is the one who trusts in the Lord, whose confidence is in Him. They will be like a tree planted by the water that sends out its roots by the stream. It does not fear when heat comes; its leaves are always green. It has no worries in a year of drought and never fails to bear fruit." (NIV)

Galatians 5:16-22, "So I say, walk by the Spirit, and you will not gratify the desires of the flesh. For the flesh desires what is contrary to the Spirit, and the Spirit what is contrary to the flesh. They are in conflict with each other, so that you are not to do whatever you want. But if you are led by the Spirit, you are not under the law. The acts of the flesh are obvious: sexual immorality, impurity and debauchery; idolatry and witchcraft; hatred, discord, jealousy, fits of rage, selfish ambition, dissensions, factions and envy; drunkenness, orgies, and the like. I warn you, as I did before, that those who live like this will not inherit the kingdom of God. But the fruit of the Spirit is love, joy, peace, forbearance, kindness, goodness, faithfulness, gentleness and self-control. Against such things there is no law. Those who belong to Christ Jesus have crucified the flesh with its passions and desires. Since we live by the Spirit, let us keep in step with the Spirit. Let us not become conceited, provoking and envying each other." (NIV)

CHAPTER 6

1 Thessalonians 4:3, "For this is the will of God, your sanctification: that you abstain from sexual immorality" (ESV)

Genesis 4:1, "And Adam knew Eve his wife..." (KJV)

Exodus 33:17, "And the LORD said to Moses, 'I will do the very thing you have asked, because I am pleased with you and I know you by name.'" (NIV)

Matthew 6:8, ".... your Father knows what you need before you ask him." (NIV)

Corinthians 8:3, "But if anyone loves God, he is known by God." (ESV)

John 10:14, "I am the good shepherd, and I know My own and My own know Me." (NASB)

John 10:27, "My sheep hear My voice, and I know them, and they follow Me." (NKJV)

Nahum 1:7, "The LORD is good, A stronghold in the day of trouble, And He knows those who take refuge in Him." (NASB)

Matthew 11:27, "All things have been handed over to me by my Father, and no one knows the Son except the Father, and no one knows the Father except the Son and anyone to whom the Son chooses to reveal him." (ESV)

John 10:15, "As the Father knows Me, even so I know the Father; and I lay down My life for the sheep." (NKJV)

Romans 7:15-20, "I do not understand what I do. For what I want to do I do not do, but what I hate I do. And if I do what I do not want to do, I agree that the law is good. As it is, it is no longer I myself who do it, but it is sin living in me. For I know that good itself does not dwell in me, that is, in my sinful nature. For I have the desire to do what is good, but I cannot carry it out. For I do not do the good I want to do, but the evil I do not want to do—this I keep on doing. Now if I do what I do not want to do, it is no longer I who do it, but it is sin living in me that does it." (NIV)

Ephesians 5:1-3, "Therefore be imitators of God, as beloved children. And walk in love, as Christ loved us and gave himself up for us, a fragrant offering and sacrifice to God. But sexual immorality and all impurity or covetousness must not even be named among you, as is proper among saints." (ESV)

1 Corinthians 6:13-20, "You say, 'Food was made for the stomach, and the stomach for food.' (This is true, though someday God will do away with both of them.) But you cannot say that our bodies were made for sexual immorality. They were made for the Lord, and the Lord cares about our bodies. And God will raise us from the dead by his power, just as he raised our Lord from the dead. Don't you realize that your bodies are actually parts of Christ? Should a man take his body, which is part of Christ, and join it to a prostitute (sexual immorality)? Never! And don't you realize that if a man joins himself to a prostitute, he becomes one body with her? For the Scriptures say, 'The two are united into one.' But the person who is joined to the Lord is one spirit with him. Run from sexual sin! No other sin so clearly affects the body as this one does. For sexual immorality is a sin against your own body. Don't you realize that your body is the temple of the Holy Spirit, who lives in you and was given to you by God? You do not belong to yourself, for God bought you with a high price. So you must honor God with your body." (NLT)

Ephesians 2:10, "For we are his workmanship, created in Christ Jesus for good works, which God prepared beforehand, that we should walk in them." (ESV)

1 Corinthians 7:8-9, "Now to the unmarried and the widows I say: It is good for them to stay unmarried, as I do. But if they cannot control themselves, they should marry, for it is better to marry than to burn with passion." (NIV)

Ephesians 5:25, "Husbands, love your wives, just as Christ loved the church and gave himself up for her" (NIV)

John 4:4-26, "Now he had to go through Samaria. So, he came to a town in Samaria called Sychar, near the plot of ground Jacob had given to his son Joseph. Jacob's well was there, and Jesus, tired as he was from the journey, sat down by the well. It was about noon. When a Samaritan woman came to draw water, Jesus said to her, 'Will you give me a drink?' (His disciples had gone into the town to buy food.) The Samaritan woman said to him, 'You are a Jew and I am a Samaritan woman. How can you ask me for a drink?' (For Jews do not associate with Samaritans.) Jesus answered her, 'If you knew the gift of God and who it is that asks you for a drink, you would have asked him and he would have given you living water.' 'Sir,' the woman said, 'you have nothing to draw with and the well is deep. Where can you get this living water? Are you greater than our father, Jacob, who gave us the well and drank from it himself, as did also his sons and his livestock?' Jesus answered, 'Everyone who drinks this water will be thirsty again, but whoever drinks the water I give them will never thirst. Indeed, the water I give them will become in them a spring of water welling up to eternal life.' The woman said to him, 'Sir, give me this water so that I won't get thirsty and have to keep coming here to draw water.' He told her, 'Go, call your husband and come back.' 'I have no husband,' she replied. Jesus said to her, 'You are right when you say you have no husband. The fact is, you have had five husbands, and the man you now have is not your husband. What you have just said is quite true.' 'Sir,' the woman said, 'I can see that you are a prophet. Our ancestors worshiped on this mountain, but you Jews claim that the place where we must worship is in Jerusalem.' 'Woman,' Jesus replied, 'believe me, a time is coming when you will worship the Father neither on this mountain nor in Jerusalem. You Samaritans worship what you do not know; we worship what we do know, for salvation is from the Jews. Yet a time is coming and has now come when the true worshipers will worship the Father in the Spirit and in truth, for they are the kind of worshipers the Father seeks. God is spirit, and his worshipers must worship in the Spirit and in truth.' The woman said, 'I know that Messiah' (called Christ) 'is coming. When he comes, he will explain everything to us.' Then Jesus declared, 'I, the one speaking to you—I am he.'" (NIV)

John 4:28-29, "Then, leaving her water jar, the woman went back to the town and said to the people, 'Come, see a man who told me everything I ever did. Could this be the Messiah?'" (NIV)

Genesis 2:24, "That is why a man leaves his father and mother and is united to his wife, and they become one flesh. Adam and his wife were both naked, and they felt no shame." (NIV)

Galatians 5:19-21, "Now the works of the flesh are evident: sexual immorality, impurity, sensuality, idolatry, sorcery, enmity, strife, jealousy, fits of anger, rivalries, dissensions, divisions, envy, drunkenness, orgies, and things like these. I warn you, as I warned you before, that those who do such things will not inherit the kingdom of God." (ESV)

1 John 2:15-17, "Do not love the world or anything in the world. If anyone loves the world, love for the Father is not in them. For everything in the world—the lust of the flesh, the lust of the eyes, and the pride of life—comes not from the Father but from the world. The world and its desires pass away, but whoever does the will of God lives forever." (NIV)

Ephesians 5:25-27, "Husbands, love your wives, just as Christ loved the church and gave himself up for her to make her holy, cleansing her by the washing with water through the word, and to present her to himself as a radiant church, without stain or wrinkle or any other blemish, but holy and blameless." (NIV)

Galatians 2:17, "But if, while we seek to be justified by Christ, we ourselves also are found sinners, is Christ therefore a minister of sin? Certainly not!" (NKJV)

Romans 8:7-9, "Our desires fight against God, because they do not and cannot obey God's laws. If we follow our desires, we cannot please God. You are no longer ruled by your desires, but by God's Spirit, who lives in you." (CEV)

Galatians 2:20, "I have been crucified with Christ. It is no longer I who live, but Christ who lives in me. And the life I now live in the flesh I live by faith in the Son of God, who loved me and gave himself for me." (ESV)

Galatians 5:16, "So I say, walk by the Spirit, and you will not gratify the desires of the flesh." (NIV)

Romans 8:9, "You are no longer ruled by your desires, but by God's Spirit, who lives in you." (CEV)

Philippians 4:6-7, "Do not worry about anything; instead, pray about everything. Tell God what you need and thank him for all he has done. Then you will experience God's peace, which exceeds anything we can understand. His peace will guard your hearts and minds as you live in Christ Jesus." (NLT)

Isaiah 26:3, "You will keep in perfect peace all who trust in you, all whose thoughts are fixed on you!" (NLT)

CHAPTER 7

Hebrews 12:15, "See to it that no one falls short of the grace of God and that no bitter root grows up to cause trouble and defile many." (NIV)

Mark 11:26, "But if you do not forgive, neither will your Father in heaven forgive your trespasses." (NKJV)

Colossians 3:13, "Bear with each other and forgive one another if any of you has a grievance against someone. Forgive as the Lord forgave you." (NIV)

Matthew 5:23-24, "Therefore, if you are offering your gift at the altar and there remember that your brother or sister has something against you, leave your gift there in front of the altar. First go and be reconciled to them; then come and offer your gift." (NIV)

John 8:36, "So if the Son sets you free, you will be free indeed." (NIV)

Matthew 6:14, "For if you forgive other people when they sin against you, your heavenly Father will also forgive you." (NIV)

Luke 23:34-37, "And Jesus was saying, 'Father, forgive them; for they do not know what they are doing.' And they cast lots, dividing his clothes among themselves. Now the people stood by, watching; but even the rulers ridiculed and sneered at Him saying, 'He saved others [from death]; let Him save Himself if He is the Christ (the Messiah, the Anointed) of God, His Chosen One.'" (AMP)

Isaiah 53:5-7, "But He was wounded for our transgressions, He was bruised for our iniquities; The chastisement for our peace was upon Him, And by His stripes we are healed. All we like sheep have gone astray; We have turned, everyone to his own way; And the Lord has laid on Him the iniquity of us all. He was oppressed and He was afflicted, Yet He opened not His mouth; He was led as a lamb to the slaughter..." (NKJV)

Matthew 27:46, "About the ninth hour Jesus cried out with a loud [agonized] voice, "ELI, ELI, LAMA SABACHTHANI?" that is, "MY GOD, MY GOD, WHY HAVE YOU FORSAKEN ME?" (AMP)

Matthew 6:14, "For if you forgive other people when they sin against you, your heavenly Father will also forgive you." (NIV)

Matthew 27:54, "When the centurion and those with him who were guarding Jesus saw the earthquake and all that had happened, they were terrified, and exclaimed, "Surely he was the Son of God!" (NIV)

Matthew 27:50-52, "And when Jesus had cried out again in a loud voice, he gave up his spirit. At that moment the curtain of the temple was torn in two from top to bottom. The earth shook, the rocks split, and the tombs broke open." (NIV)

Psalms 16:10, "For thou wilt not leave my soul in hell; neither wilt thou suffer thine Holy One to see corruption." (KJV)

Acts 2:27, "For you will not leave my soul in Hades, nor will You allow Your Holy One to see corruption." (NKJV)

Ephesians 4:9-10, "(Now this, 'He ascended'—what does it mean but that He also first descended into the lower parts of the earth? He who descended is also the One who ascended far above all the heavens, that He might fill all things.) (NKJV)

1 Peter 3:18-20, "For indeed Christ died for sins once for all, the Just and Righteous for the unjust and unrighteous [the Innocent for the guilty] so that He might bring us to God, having been put to death in the flesh, but made alive in the Spirit; in which He also went and preached to the spirits now in prison, who once were disobedient, when the great patience of God was waiting in the days of Noah, during the building of the ark, in which a few, that is, eight persons [Noah's family], were brought safely through the water." (AMP)

Revelation 1:17-18, "When I saw him, I fell at his feet as though dead. Then he placed his right hand on me and said: 'Do not be afraid. I am the First and the Last. I am the Living One; I was dead, and now look, I am alive for ever and ever! And I hold the keys of death and Hades.'" (NIV)

Isaiah 53:4-6, "Surely He has borne our griefs and carried our sorrows; Yet we esteemed Him stricken, smitten by God, and afflicted. But He was wounded for our transgressions, He was bruised for our iniquities; the chastisement for our peace was upon Him, and by His stripes we are healed. All we like sheep have gone astray; We have turned, every one, to his own way; And the Lord has laid on Him the iniquity of us all." (NKJV)

Matthew 5:45, "For he gives his sunlight to both the evil and the good, and he sends rain on the just and the unjust alike." (NLT)

CHAPTER 8

Philippians 3:13, "Brothers and sisters, I do not consider that I have made it my own yet, but one thing I do: forgetting what lies behind and reaching forward to what lies ahead" (AMP)

Romans 8:1-2, "Therefore, there is now no condemnation for those who are in Christ Jesus, because through Christ Jesus the law of the Spirit who gives life has set you free from the law of sin and death." (NIV)

Genesis 19:17, "When they had brought them outside, one [of the angels] said, 'Escape for your life! Do not look behind you or stop anywhere in the entire valley; escape to the mountains [of Moab], or you will be consumed and swept away.'" (AMP)

Genesis 19:24-26, "Then the Lord rained down brimstone (flaming sulfur) and fire on Sodom and on Gomorrah from the Lord out of heaven, and He overthrew (demolished, ended) those cities, and the entire valley, and all the inhabitants of the cities, and whatever grew on the ground. But Lot's wife, from behind him, [foolishly, longingly] looked [back toward Sodom in an act of disobedience], and she became a pillar of salt." (AMP)

Philippians 3:13-14, "Brothers and Sisters I do not consider that I have made it my own yet; but one thing I do: forgetting what lies behind and reaching forward to what lies ahead, I press on toward the goal to win the [heavenly] prize of the upward call of God in Christ Jesus." (AMP)

Psalms 40:2, "He lifted me out of the slimy pit, out of the mud and mire; he set my feet on a rock and gave me a firm place to stand." (NIV)

Philippians 4:6-7, "Be anxious for nothing, but in everything by prayer and supplication, with thanksgiving, let your requests be made known to God; and the peace of God, which surpasses all understanding, will guard your hearts and minds through Christ Jesus." (NKJV)

Philippians 4:13, "I can do all things through Christ who strengthens me." (KJV)

Ephesians 2:10, "For we are God's handiwork, created in Christ Jesus to do good works," (NIV)

Proverbs 29:10 says, "Where there is no vision, the people perish: but he that keepeth the law, happy is he." (KJV)

Matthew 7:11, "If you then, being evil, know how to give good gifts to your children, how much more will your Father who is in heaven give good things to those who ask Him!" (NIV)

Matthew 6:10, "Thy will be done on earth, as it is in heaven." (NKJV)

2 Corinthians 5:21, "God made him who had no sin to be sin for us, so that in Him we might become the righteousness of God." (NIV)

Acts 16:26, "At once all the prison doors flew open, and everyone's chains came loose." (NIV)

Hebrews 13:5, "...*Never will I leave you; never will I forsake you.*" (NIV)

Psalms 138:8, *"The Lord will accomplish that which concerns me; Your lovingkindness, O Lord, endures forever..."* (AMP)

Matthew 7:7, *"Ask, and it will be given to you; seek, and you will find; knock, and it will be opened to you;"* (NIV)

John 14:13, *"And whatever you ask in My name, that I will do, that the Father may be glorified in the Son. If you ask anything in My name, I will do it."* (NKJV)

Philippians 1:6, *"Being confident of this very thing, that He who has begun a good work in you will complete it until the day of Jesus Christ."* (NKJV)

Acts 16:25-27, *"Around midnight Paul and Silas were praying and singing hymns to God, and the other prisoners were listening. Suddenly, there was a massive earthquake, and the prison was shaken to its foundations. All the doors immediately flew open, and the chains of every prisoner fell off! The jailer woke up to see the prison doors wide open."* (NLT)

Isaiah 43:18-19, *"Do not remember the former things, nor consider the things of old. Behold, I will do a new thing, now it shall spring forth; Shall you not know it? I will even make a road in the wilderness and rivers in the desert."* (NKJV)

Genesis 35:3, *"Then come, let us go up to Bethel, where I will build an altar to God, who answered me in the day of my distress and who has been with me wherever I have gone."* (NIV)

1 Samuel 30:6, *"And David was greatly distressed; for the people spake of stoning him, because the soul of all the people was grieved, every man for his sons and for his daughters: but David encouraged himself in the Lord his God."* (NKJV)

Isaiah 9:4, *"For God will break the chains that bind his people and the whip that scourges them..."* (TLB)

Psalms 107:10-16, *"Some sat in darkness, in utter darkness, prisoners suffering in iron chains, because they rebelled against God's commands and despised the plans of* the Most-High. So, he subjected them to bitter labor; they stumbled, and there was no one to help. Then they cried to the Lord in their trouble, and he saved them from their distress. He brought them out of darkness, the utter darkness, and broke away their chains. Let them give thanks to the Lord for his unfailing love and his wonderful deeds for mankind, for he breaks down gates of bronze and cuts through bars of iron." (NIV)

1 Corinthians 10:13, "The temptations in your life are no different from what others experience. And God is faithful. He will not allow the temptation to be more than you can stand. When you are tempted, he will show you a way out so that you can endure." (NLT)

Hebrews 3:7-8, "Therefore, as the Holy Spirit says: 'Today, if you hear His voice, do not harden your hearts, as you did in the rebellion...'" (NIV)

James 4:7, "Submit yourselves, then, to God. Resist the devil, and he will flee from you." (NIV)

Matthew 11:28-30, "Come to me, all you who are weary and burdened, and I will give you rest. Take my yoke upon you and learn from me, for I am gentle and humble in heart, and you will find rest for your souls. For my yoke is easy and my burden is light." (NIV)

CHAPTER 9

Ephesians 2:4-5, "But God, being rich in mercy, because of the great love with which he loved us even when we were dead in our trespasses, made us alive together with Christ— by grace you have been saved." (ESV)

John 1:27, "He is the one who comes after me, the straps of whose sandals I am not worthy to untie." (NIV)

1 Corinthians 2:9, "Eye has not seen, nor ear heard, nor have entered into the heart of man, the things God has prepared for those who love Him." (NKJV)

Romans 12:2, "Do not conform to the pattern of this world, but be transformed by the renewing of your mind. Then you will be able to test and approve what God's will is--his good, pleasing and perfect will." *(NIV)*

1 John 3:1, "See what great love the Father has lavished on us, that we should be called children of God! And that is what we are!" *(NIV)*

John 3:16, "For God so loved the world that he gave his one and only Son, that whoever believes in him shall not perish but have eternal life." *(NIV)*

2 Corinthians 12:9, "My grace is sufficient for you, for my power is made perfect in weakness. Therefore I will boast all the more gladly of my weaknesses, so that the power of Christ may rest upon me." *(NIV)*

Ephesians 2:8, "For by grace you have been saved through faith. And this is not your own doing; it is the gift of God." *(ESV)*

Isaiah 53:6, "All we like sheep have gone astray; We have turned, every one, to his own way; And the Lord has laid on Him the iniquity of us all." *(NIV)*

2 Corinthians 5:17, "Therefore, if anyone is in Christ, he is a new creation; old things have passed away; behold, all things have become new." *(NKJV)*

John 3:1-8, "There was a man of the Pharisees named Nicodemus, a ruler of the Jews. This man came to Jesus by night and said to Him, "Rabbi, we know that You are a teacher come from God; for no one can do these signs that You do unless God is with him." Jesus answered and said to him, "Most assuredly, I say to you, unless one is born [a]again, he cannot see the kingdom of God." Nicodemus said to Him, "How can a man be born when he is old? Can he enter a second time into his mother's womb and be born?" Jesus answered, "Most assuredly, I say to you, unless one is born of water and the Spirit, he cannot enter the kingdom of God. That which is born of the flesh is flesh, and that which is born of the Spirit is spirit. Do not marvel that I said to you, 'You must be born again.' The wind blows where it wishes, and you hear the sound of it, but cannot tell where it comes from and where it goes. So is everyone who is born of the Spirit." *(NKJV)*

2 Corinthians 5:17, "Therefore, if anyone is in Christ, he is a new creation; old things have passed away; behold, all things have become new." (NKJV)
Revelation 12:9-10, "So the great dragon was cast out, that serpent of old, called the Devil and Satan, who deceives the whole world; he was cast to the earth, and his angels were cast out with him. Then I heard a loud voice saying in heaven, 'Now salvation, and strength, and the kingdom of our God, and the power of His Christ have come, for the accuser of our brethren, who accused them before our God day and night, has been cast down.'" (NKJV)

Isaiah 43:18, "Remember not the former things, nor consider the things of old. Behold, I am doing a new thing; now it springs forth, do you not perceive it? I will make a way in the wilderness and rivers in the desert." (NKJV)

Revelations 21:5, "Then He who sat on the throne said, 'Behold, I make all things new.'" (NKJV)

John 11:44, "The dead man came out, his hands and feet wrapped with strips of linen, and a cloth around his face. Jesus said to them, 'Take off the grave clothes and let him go.'" (NIV)

Ephesians 4:22-24, "to put off your old self, which belongs to your former manner of life and is corrupt through deceitful desires, and to be renewed in the spirit of your minds, and to put on the new self, created after the likeness of God in true righteousness and holiness." (ESV)

Colossians 3:1-10, "Since you have been raised to new life with Christ, set your sights on the realities of heaven, where Christ sits in the place of honor at God's right hand. Think about the things of heaven, not the things of earth. For you died to this life, and your real life is hidden with Christ in God. And when Christ, who is your life, is revealed to the whole world, you will share in all His glory. So put to death the sinful, earthly things lurking within you. Have nothing to do with sexual immorality, impurity, lust, and evil desires. Don't be greedy, for a greedy person is an idolater, worshiping the things of this world. Because of these sins, the anger of God is coming. You used to do these things when your life was still part of this world. But now is the time to get rid of anger, rage, malicious behavior, slander, and dirty language. Don't lie to each other, for you have stripped off your old sinful nature and all its wicked deeds. Put on your new nature and be renewed as you learn to know your Creator and become like him." *(NLT)*

Matthew 6:33, *"But seek first the kingdom of God and His righteousness, and all these things shall be added to you." (ESV)*

Galatians 5:22-25, *"But the fruit of the Spirit is love, joy, peace, patience, kindness, goodness, faithfulness, gentleness, self-control; against such things there is no law. And those who belong to Christ Jesus have crucified the flesh with its passions and desires. If we live by the Spirit, let us also keep in step with the Spirit." (ESV)*

Isaiah 65:17, *"For behold, I create new heavens and a new earth; And the former shall not be remembered or come to mind." (NKJV)*

Revelation 22:1, *"And he showed me a pure river of water of life, clear as crystal, proceeding from the throne of God and of the Lamb." (NKJV)*

Proverbs 23:7, *"For as he thinks in his heart, so is he." (NKJV)*

2 Timothy 4:3-4, *"For the time will come when people will not put up with sound doctrine. Instead, to suit their own desires, they will gather around them a great number of teachers to say what their itching ears want to hear. They will turn their ears away from the truth and turn aside to myths." (NIV)*

Revelation 22:1, *"And he showed me a [a]pure river of water of life, clear as crystal, proceeding from the throne of God and of the Lamb." (NKJV)*

Hebrews 4:12, *"For the word of God is alive and active. Sharper than any double-edged sword, it penetrates even to dividing soul and spirit, joints and marrow; it judges the thoughts and attitudes of the heart." (NIV)*

John 6:32-35, *"Then Jesus said to them, 'Most assuredly, I say to you, Moses did not give you the bread from heaven, but My Father gives you the true bread from heaven. For the bread of God is He who comes down from heaven and gives life to the world. Then they said to Him, 'Lord, give us this bread always.' And Jesus said to them, 'I am the bread of life. He who comes to Me shall never hunger, and he who believes in Me shall never thirst.'" (NKJV)*

Proverbs 4:20-27, *"My son, give attention to my words; Incline your ear to my sayings. Do not let them depart from your eyes; Keep them in the midst of your heart; For they are life to those who find them, and health to all their flesh. Keep your heart with all diligence, for out of it spring the issues of life. Put away from you a deceitful mouth and put perverse lips far from you. Let your eyes look straight ahead, and your eyelids look right before you. Ponder the path of your feet and let all your ways be established. Do not turn to the right or the left. Remove your foot from evil." (NKJV)*

1 Thessalonians 5:17-18, *"Rejoice always, pray continually, give thanks in all circumstances; for this is God's will for you in Christ Jesus." (NIV)*

Matthew 7:9-11, *"Which of you, if your son asks for bread, will give him a stone? Or if he asks for a fish, will give him a snake? If you, then, though you are evil, know how to give good gifts to your children, how much more will your Father in heaven give good gifts to those who ask him!" (NIV)*

John 4:1, *"Dear friends, do not believe every spirit, but test the spirits to see whether they are from God, because many false prophets have gone out into the world." (NIV)*

CHAPTER 10

Ephesians 2:10, *"For we are God's masterpiece. He has created us anew in Christ Jesus, so we can do the good things he planned for us long ago." (NLT)*

Job 8:7, *"Though your beginning was small, yet your latter end would increase abundantly." (NKJV)*

Ecclesiastes 3:11, *"He has made everything beautiful in its time. He has also set eternity in the human heart; yet no one can fathom what God has done from beginning to end." (NIV)*

Genesis 45:4, *"'Please, come closer,'" he said to them. So, they came closer. And he said again, 'I am Joseph, your brother, whom you sold into slavery in Egypt. But don't* be upset, and don't be angry with yourselves for selling me to this place. It was God who sent me here ahead of you to preserve your lives.'" (NLT)

Genesis 50: 19- 21, "But Joseph said to them, 'Do not be afraid. Am I in the place of God? You intended to harm me, but God intended it for good to accomplish what is now being done, the saving of many lives. So then, do not be afraid. I will provide for you and your children.' And he reassured them and spoke kindly to them." (NIV)

Psalms 115:14-15, "The Lord shall increase you more and more, you and your children." (KJV)

Psalms 16:5-6, "O Lord, You are the portion of my inheritance and my cup; You maintain my lot. The lines have fallen to me in pleasant places; Yes, I have a good inheritance." (NKJV)

Jeremiah 29:11, "'For I know the plans I have for you,' declares the Lord, 'plans to prosper you and not to harm you, plans to give you hope and a future. Then you will call on me and come and pray to me, and I will listen to you. You will seek me and find me when you seek me with all your heart. I will be found by you,' declares the Lord, 'and will bring you back from captivity. I will gather you from all the nations and places where I have banished you,' declares the Lord, 'and will bring you back to the place from which I carried you into exile.'" (NIV)

John 6:18-21, "A strong wind was blowing and the waters grew rough. When they had rowed about three or four miles, they saw Jesus approaching the boat, walking on the water; and they were frightened. But he said to them, 'It is I; do not be afraid.' Then they were willing to take him into the boat, and immediately the boat reached the shore where they were heading." (NIV)

Psalms 30:11-12, "You have turned my mourning into dancing for me; You have taken off my sackcloth and clothed me with joy..." (AMP)

John 3:16-17, "For God so loved the world that he gave his one and only Son, that whoever believes in him shall not perish but have eternal life. For God did not send his Son into the world to condemn the world, but to save the world through him." (NIV)

Philippians 4:8, "Finally, brethren, whatsoever things are true, whatsoever things are honest, whatsoever things are just, whatsoever things are pure, whatsoever things are lovely, whatsoever things are of good report; if there be any virtue, and if there be any praise, think on these things." (KJV)

205

Psalms 103:12, "as far as the east is from the west, so far has he removed our transgressions from us." (NIV) And Hebrews 8:12 tells us He remembers them no more, "For I will be merciful to their unrighteousness, and their sins and their iniquities will I remember no more." (KJV)

Hebrews 8:12 tells us He remembers them no more, "For I will be merciful to their unrighteousness, and their sins and their iniquities will I remember no more." (KJV)

John 10:27-30, "My sheep hear my voice, and I know them, and they follow me. I give them eternal life, and they will never perish, and no one will snatch them out of my hand. My Father, who has given them to me, is greater than all, and no one is able to snatch them out of the Father's hand. I and the Father are one." (ESV)

Mark 16:15, "Go into all the world and preach the gospel to all creation." (NIV)

Mark 6:3-6, "'Isn't this the carpenter? Isn't this Mary's son and the brother of James, Joseph, Judas, and Simon? Aren't his sisters here with us?' And they took offense at him. Jesus said to them, 'A prophet is not without honor except in his own town, among his relatives and in his own home.' He could not do any miracles there, except lay his hands on a few sick people and heal them. He was amazed at their lack of faith." (NIV)

Luke 4:24, "'Truly I tell you,' He continued, 'no prophet is accepted in his hometown.'" (NIV)

Revelation 12:10-11, "Then I heard a loud voice saying in heaven, "Now salvation, and strength, and the kingdom of our God, and the power of His Christ have come, for the accuser of our brethren, who accused them before our God day and night, has been cast down. And they overcame him by the blood of the Lamb and by the word of their testimony, and they did not love their lives to the death." (NKJV)

Mark 16:15, "Go into all the world and preach the gospel to every creature." (NIV)

2 Chronicles 15:7, "But as for you, be strong and do not give up, for your work will be rewarded." (NIV)

Notes

CHAPTER 3: It's Dark in Here

1. "National Right to Life Releases Ninth Annual Report: The State of Abortion in the United States," *nrlc.org*, January 31, 2022. https://www.nrlc.org/communications/releases/2022/013122sausreport/..

CHAPTER 8: Forgetting what Lies Behind

2. "How did a Decapitated Snake Bite Itself?" *National Geographic,* August 16, 2013. https://blog.nationalgeographic.org/2013/08/16/how-did-a-decapitated-snake-bite-itself/

9 781733 930598